G. Rosemary L

Freedom

Crystal Journals 4

G. Rosemary Ludlow

This is a work of fiction. All of the characters, organizations, and events portrayed in this novel are either the products of the author's imagination or are used fictitiously.

1. Juvenile Fiction. 2. Fantasy & Magic 3. Space Travel 4. Future 5. Teamwork

Summary: Young time traveler, Susan Sinclair, one of the "Crystal Guardians", is transported into the future - 2256. She is the catalyst in helping a group of children and others in their struggle for freedom against almost overwhelming odds.

Cover Art by Ken Rolston

Library and Archives Canada Cataloging in Publication
ISBN-13: 978-0973687170
ISBN-10: 0973687170eBook
ISBN: 9780973687187

Published by:
Comwave Publishing House Inc.
2751 Oxford Street,
Vancouver, BC V5K 1N5

For
all those who seek
Freedom.

Freedom for
themselves and for
others.

Freedom

THE STORY SO FAR

Book 1, A Rare Gift, tells the story of how Susan Sinclair is chosen by the Crystal of the North to be its Guardian. Susan later learns that there are four crystals and that hers will lead her to places where there is an imbalance or unfairness in the world and that she will be able to help correct the situation.

Susan gradually grows into her Guardian role and has many adventures helping immigrant children sailing to New York in the 1860s. Along the way she learns to take pride in her crystal. She grows in confidence. She learns that she can help people and that she enjoys doing so.

Book 2, Pharaoh's Tomb. As Susan travels back through time her crystal fades from her hand. She arrives in Ancient Egypt with no crystal to take her back to her family.

A magician has pulled her into his time to help him create the crystals. She is in a time before her crystal was formed. Her only way home is to work with this ambitious and self-centered man to create the crystals. While the crystals are growing Susan lives as a princess within the court of the pharaoh, Tuthmoses II. She makes friends and foes as she learns to live in this totally different culture.

By the time her crystal is fully formed and calling to her, tragedy has moved it far beyond her reach. She must show courage and resolution to retrieve her crystal and bid her new friends goodbye.

Book 3, Lady Knight, Susan and her cousin Jason time slip to the year 1212. They find themselves in Medieval Europe. They meet children traveling to join the Children's Crusade. Hidden among them is a royal runaway. She has information very important to her family and is being pursued by knights who will stop at nothing to capture her. Susan, Jason and others join together to bring the runaway safely to her family.

And now onto Book 4, Freedom.

1

It's a Birthday . . . Surprise!

Susan jiggled the handle three times, then pushed. The toilet flushed. She always did that in the powder room at Judy's place. She sashayed over to the wash basin, then chuckled as she squished the lavender hand wash onto her palm. *They tricked me with a surprise party*. She smiled and rubbed up a good lather. As she rinsed her hands, her feet danced in place. Susan felt good. Her smile was so wide her cheeks felt crunched.

That's when her crystal, thrust deep in her pocket, gave a little tingle.

"Oh no, Crystal, not now. It's my eleventh birthday surprise party. I can't leave now. I don't have my travel bag with me."

Her crystal zapped her leg. "Ouch." Susan reached for the hand towel.

The door burst open. Judy stood in the doorway. "I figured you'd be here," she said. "We're all ready to light your candles." Judy beckoned. "Come on."

"I locked the door."

Judy shrugged. "Darren and I figured out how to bump the lock years ago."

Susan peered at Judy. Her yellow t-shirt was beginning to smear. *Oh no.*

Judy held her hand out. "Susan, you're getting blurry."

In desperation, Susan pushed Judy out of the room and slammed the door in her face. She locked it again.

"Suuuuusannnnn!" Judy exclaimed.

"I'll be fine, Judy." Susan stuttered. "Just give me a minute. OK? It's . . . it's all been a little overwhelming. I'll be out in a minute."

"OK. I'll get everyone ready." Judy sighed. The last thing Susan heard was the back door slamming as Judy went outside.

Then she went.

2

Two Crystals?

B*lack*

Nothing.

Susan sniffed.

The air felt cooler than home, like the first mornings of fall. Another breath. It smelled like nothing she'd ever smelt before. Not bad, not good—just different.

Susan took a long, deep breath. She could breathe.

Could she see?

Were her eyes open?

She touched her fingers gently to her eyes.

Yes, open. She peered into the utter blackness.

Nothing.

Sounds?

What could she hear?

Nothing.

No. Wait. A low hum. She could barely hear it. No changes to the sound. Just a background hum. No, the sound was all around her. She had to strain her ears to even hear it. *I could be imagining it. Maybe my ears are filling in for the nothingness. Maybe I'm between places. I was scared something like this could happen when I first jumped to Lady Beatrice.*

Susan shuddered all over. *But,* she reminded herself, *my crystal has never dropped me in an unsafe place before*. Susan shuddered again. *This is really creepy*.

Susan sighed.

Crystal, where have you brought me? Crystal?

Susan felt at her pocket. She couldn't feel her crystal.

She checked all her pockets. No crystal. *Not again!*

She held out her hand. "Crystal, come to me," she ordered out loud.

Whack! Her crystal landed on her palm. She closed her fingers around it in relief.

Whack! Something hit her knuckles.

She felt with her other hand. What had hit her? *It feels . . . it feels like . . . another crystal.*

She lay the two on her palm.

Her crystal danced with light. And in the sparkle, Susan could see the new crystal. It was the same shape but looked blue. Susan held them close to her face. Her crystal glowed with light, but the blue one just looked like a blue crystal. When she peered really close, she thought she might be able to see a teeny-tiny spark of sapphire deep within.

This crystal must have powers too. It came when I called. I wonder if it has a Guardian.

Her crystal shimmied across her palm until it connected with the sapphire one. There, it stuck. Susan tried to pull them apart, but they were inseparable. Something about a blue crystal niggled at the back of her mind. She tried to grab the thought. But, no, it was gone.

Using the small amount of light from the Crystal of the North, Susan tried looking around again. All black. It didn't feel as though she was in a vast space, but she could see no walls and no light.

"Crystal," she held it tight, "take me back to the exact moment when I locked the door of the powder room."

She waited for the smearing. She waited to go.

Nothing.

Susan sighed. "Well, I guess there's something here I need to do."

"Hello," she called. "Is there anyone here? . . . I've arrived

Silence.

But, the background hum sounded a little louder.

Warning. Warning. Warning.

Establishing light.

Earth, Morning.

Now!

Lights came on.

3

Stuck

Susan squinted against the sudden light. She peered around. *Walls!* She was in a round room. She scuttled across the floor until her back pressed against a wall. Feeling safer, she began carefully examining her surroundings.

The dark gray walls arched above her. *It's like a cave.*

She stroked the floor. It felt like smooth stone or maybe tiles. *Well then, not a cave.*

Solid stone walls were all around her. She saw no door.

Trapped.

Susan took a deep breath, trying to calm herself. She gulped. It felt like she needed to swallow her heart. Blood drummed in her ears.

Calm down, she ordered herself. *Panicking won't help. The crystal brought me here for a reason, so there must be a way out. I just have to find it.*

This place felt different to any other place she had ever been. She couldn't explain it.

There's the low hum and almost . . . sort of . . . a vibration?

Susan wasn't sure. She laid her hand gently on the rock. Yes, she could feel a slight vibration under her fingertips.

Susan shut her eyes and moved her other senses out, picking up clues as to what felt familiar about this feeling. The quiet, persistent, throb; the slight vibration. And then she had it.

Once on a trip across the strait to Vancouver, she felt tired, so her family stayed in their car for the ferry ride. As she slowly awoke from her snooze, with her eyes still closed, she had sensed the ferry around her—a background hum and a slight vibration.

But, on the ferry there had been people noises as well. And the movement of the ship traveling across Georgia Strait. In this stony room, Susan could hear no other sounds, and there was no feeling of movement.

My crystal brought me here. There must be someone here I can help.

"Hello," she whispered. "I'm here. I've come to help." Susan looked around. "Where am I?"

Nothing. Nothing changed.

Susan slumped back against the wall. *Eleven years old today and I didn't even get birthday cake.*

With nothing to look at and nothing to do, Susan finally lay out on the floor. She worked through every stretching exercise she knew and did her deep breathing exercises as well.

Apart from the slight unknown scent, the air felt the same as always. She thought back through her experiences. *Huh, air does smell different in each place.* She thought of home, with the sun shining on the pine trees, that was one type of smell. Then there was the smell of the rivers—a bit muddy, a bit fishy. And then she remembered the smell of the dungeon in Cologne. She let out a sigh. At least this rocky room didn't stink.

Next Susan moved carefully along the walls. Maybe there was a door she couldn't see or a hidden lever or button. She reached up as high as she could. She poked and prodded at the walls. She peered into crevasses in the rock. Nothing.

She was locked in a cave-like room and didn't know where or why. Susan shook her head.

Finally, tired, hungry and discouraged, Susan slumped to the floor. She shut her eyes, just for a moment, and fell asleep.

4

Sassy

Susan woke to the strange feeling of something touching her arm with light cold strokes.

She tried to move; she tried to stop breathing. The touches felt soft and gentle. Someone or something was touching her.

Still pretending to be asleep, Susan sighed and rolled over. She opened her eyes just a fraction at the same time. There was a box standing next to her. A box with one arm unfolded from its side. This arm was patting her arm.

"We know you are awake, Crystal Keeper."

Susan sat up and rubbed her eyes.

She looked at a box. As she moved, the box retracted its arm, which folded tight against its side.

"Your heart rate has risen alarmingly. Is this normal for you?"

The voice came from the box, but Susan could see no mouth moving or a speaker grid. A whirring noise, like a small electric motor, sounded and the box moved away from her a little.

A row of small lights shone out about two inches down from the top. They appeared to go right around. The box stood about a yard square. It was all gray.

"Is it normal for you to have an empty stomach and be lacking water?"

Susan shook her head. "No. I am hungry and thirsty." She peered closely at the box. "Are you a robot?"

"I am a Semi-stealth Autonomous Storage Device." A lid popped open on the top of the box. Susan smelled food. She rose onto her knees and peered in

A roll nestled on a plate inside. Susan picked it up. It smelled freshly baked. She looked to see what else was there. She saw green stuff that looked like it could be a salad green. Then she noticed purple stuff in juice. Pickled beets. She added that to her bun. Cheese slices came next. "Is there any tomato?"

"None were harvested in time. Would you like to wait?"

"Um, well not right now if you don't have any." Susan shut the lid and sat with her back against the wall. "This will be fine."

The Semi-stealth Autonomous Storage Device moved closer. A flap opened on the side and a little tray pushed out. "You require fluid."

Susan took the little cup from the tray and sniffed it. It smelled like water. She took a sip. Yes, water. The little sip made her thirst for more. Susan gulped the little cup dry. She replaced it on the tray, and it retracted and shot straight out again with the cup full of water.

Susan sat back, sipped her drink, and chomped on her salad roll.

The box sat still, not moving.

She noticed that one little flap on the side of the Semi-stealth Autonomous Storage Device was broken. The flap was dented along one side and didn't close tight. There was a small cavity in behind the flap.

"What happened there?" she asked, waving her roll at the empty space.

"Something I had for safe-keeping was forcibly wrested from me."

"Goodness, did it hurt?"

"I am a Semi-stealth Autonomous Storage Device. I don't feel things like a human would, but I do not like to lose things that were entrusted to me."

"What was taken?"

"A sapphire blue crystal. A very important blue crystal."

Susan quirked her face. She dug deep into the pocket of her jeans. She brought out the two crystals, hers and the blue one. "You mean this blue one?"

"Yes, yes, give it back."

"OK." Susan tugged at the crystals. They wouldn't part.

"Crystal, release the blue crystal," she ordered.

The two clung together.

The Semi-stealth Autonomous Storage Device reached out its arm and gently touched the two crystals. "They must belong together."

Susan reached out her hand to the device. "I think you and I are going to be working together here. Let's be friends."

"I've never had a friend."

"Well, there's a first time for everything."

Susan grabbed the arm and gave it a shake.

"My name is Susan Sinclair, and I am the Guardian of the Crystal of the North."

The device shook her hand. "I am a Semi-stealth Autonomous Storage Device, and I was safe-keeping the Crystal of the Outer Regions."

Susan shook her head. "I can't keep calling you by that long name. What do people call you?"

"I could have a name?"

"Hmm, well, let's see. Semi-stealth, that's an S . . . Autonomous, that's an A . . . Storage, that's an S . . . SAS. I'm going to call you Sassy. Is that all right?

"You've given me a name." Sassy twirled in place. Its lights flashed bright blue.

5

Meet the Partition

Get on with it. She's fed. Get her to Control Room B.

Sassy stopped in mid twirl.

"Er, right. We're on our way."

It turned to Susan. "Come on. We have to go."

Susan stood. "Go where? I don't even know where I am."

"Come on. The partition is very particular about getting you started. We have to hurry."

"How long have I been here?"

"Two hours, sixteen minutes, forty-three seconds, forty-four seconds, forty-five-sec. . ."

"Stop, I get the idea. You don't have to keep counting down."

"Oh, right." Sassy turned and charged straight at the wall. "Here we go."

Susan waited for the smash, but it never came. As Sassy reached the wall, a space folded in on itself, and Sassy sped through.

Susan ran over and knelt to have a look. The gap was just a few centimeters wider than Sassy. She could see the robot's lights proceeding along a tunnel, which was not getting any wider. Susan sighed and crawled in after Sassy.

***

It was slow going. *I'm glad I've got jeans on. At least my knees are protected.*

She slogged on. At first, Sassy's sound moved away from her, but then she heard it getting louder. Sassy returned.

"You're slow. Is that how people move on your world?"

Susan sat back to have a rest. "No, actually we walk upright." She thought a moment. "What do you mean 'on your world'? Where am I?"

"Oh, erm . . ." Sassy reversed quickly and zipped off along the tunnel. "Come as fast as you can," it called back to her.

Susan sighed and began crawling again. *At least the floor is smooth.*

***

Finally, Susan saw light. She sighed with relief and crawled on.

She heard voices ahead.

You brought her through the service tunnel!

"Erm . . ."

Dolt. What I have to work with!

Susan sat quietly to listen.

Why didn't you fold the main doors? This person could have walked here in half the time. I have secured this area. There is no oversight here.

"The service tunnel was the shortest way."

Susan heard Sassy's little wheels whirring back and forth.

"She will be here soon, I think."

You can enter the room now, Susan Sinclair, Guardian of the Crystal of the North.

Susan crawled out into a well-lit room. She stood and slowly stretched to give herself a chance to look around. She needed time to assess the situation. The walls were the same type of rock, but here she saw a few streaks of red and copper within the gray. Like the other room, the floor was smooth and polished. The walls looked rough. Susan walked across the room when she noticed a patch of smoothness. She reached out her hand to feel.

Don't get fingerprints all over the screen.

Susan heard a tut-tutting noise.

Really.

Susan pulled her hand back.

The most surprising thing was that only Sassy occupied the room with her.

"Who's speaking?" she asked. "Why are you ordering me around?" Susan put her hands on her hips and stuck out her chin. "And," she added, "where is here?"

Feisty. I like that.

"I came here because something needs fixing, so why don't you come out and explain the problem to me instead of playing silly games behind the wall." Susan glared around.

Now, dear. Calm yourself. All will be explained. Semi-stealth Autonomous Storage Device, plug in. Do it!

"I'm called Sassy now."

Really? Sigh. We're waiting.

"Plugging in." Sassy sped over to the wall screen. A small hatch flipped open in its side and a cord snaked out and fitted into a connector beside the screen.

"Activating." The screen lit.

Susan sank cross-legged to the floor to watch.

At last some answers.

6

Some Answers

The screen showed a hand. As it pulled back, Susan saw that blood covered most of the fingertips.

"Are you recording?" a gaspy voice asked.

"Yes, Sirrah." That was Sassy's reply.

A man lay slumped on mossy ground, his back against a tree. Susan heard birds singing and, somewhere further away, the drumming of a woodpecker.

What really caught her attention, though, was the man. His hand was now firmly clasped to his chest, but blood slowly seeped through his fingers.

"I don't think I have much time." He gasped. "I must leave something for the one who will come next."

Susan nodded, her eyes glued to the screen.

"My name is Alvion True. I am the Keeper of the Crystal of the Outer Regions. May the next Keeper, you, have more luck with this problem than I."

Alvion waved his other arm to indicate the forest around him. It was obvious to Susan that even that small gesture caused him pain.

"Something is wrong here," Alvion continued. "My crystal brought me to this place, so there must be an imbalance . . . but I could not find one. Look at me, you that comes next. I've been murdered here. . . . Something is definitely wrong. You must find it. This place is important and needs saving. All the peoples of the solar system . . . need this place to flourish and prosper."

Susan gulped. *The Solar System?!*

Alvion continued, "I have enhanced this autonomous storage device to become semi stealth. It will cloak your intrusion.

"I also partitioned a segment of the system AI . . . which I could use separate from the whole. The partition and the device will work together. . . . For secrecy, they communicate through a closed network which bypasses the overall wireless system. I have informed them to expect someone . . . to arrive in my place."

Susan watched as Alvion tried to find a more comfortable position. Each time he moved, more blood welled out between his fingers. Susan reached out her hand to help, but knew she couldn't get to this man. She clasped her hands tightly in her lap.

Alvion spoke on. "The final shipment of mammals arrived. I heard the airlock doors open and close. I went to . . . greet the crew. I thought that maybe they were having trouble.

"I saw two of them dumping cages out of the ship. . . . Cages small and large were scattered all around the airlock. They didn't look like people who should be entrusted with the care of rare animals. Two of them were rough and ready. The third was . . . working on the computer console in the corner of the cargo bay.

"I watched. I didn't approach. . . . It looked like they could be the problem.

"I moved down into the biosphere to collect my thoughts. The animals must be protected here. It is a beautiful place. . . . It will be valuable to all our lives.

"But now I am murdered . . . so something must be happening that I don't understand. And now I will not be able to settle the imbalance.

"Be extremely cautious. . . . I must have triggered some surveillance system. I was shot with a projectile weapon. These are . . . not used on space stations or in the domes of Mars and the Moon. Only Earthers use weapons that can pierce structure. If it had been a laser strike, it would have cauterized and I wouldn't be bleeding so badly.

"Take care, you who follows me. This was not a warning shot. . . . This was a kill shot. I will soon be dead.

"I have stowed my crystal in one of the compartments on this storage device. . . . You will find it. The instructions for its use are in my office on the 14th level of Green Area, Room 443C. Please inform my family of my passing. . . . They are many on Clarion's Cry. Tell them I love them. . . . Please. Good luck. Stop recording."

The screen went black.

7

More Answers Needed

Susan leaped to her feet, her fists clasped to her sides. This Guardian was dead. Murdered.

He'd come to help and been shot.

Susan was angry. She had been in danger before, but this man, Alvion True, had died. Not by accident. Someone had deliberately killed him.

This put another whole layer onto her life. She had two tasks now. Fix the problem that had brought Alvion True to this place; and find out who killed him and bring them to justice. Susan sucked in a huge breath. *I'm eleven. How am I supposed to do that?*

And where was she anyway?

She was in tunnels, but Alvion was slumped against a tree in a forest, and he spoke as though it was the same place.

"Sassy, did Alvion die?"

"Yes."

"What happened to his body?" Susan began to pace the room, jerking her fists in front of her.

"It was buried."

"How long ago did he die?" "Five hours, twenty-two minutes, and sixteen seconds." Susan whirled and pointed at Sassy. "Don't start counting seconds again."

"I wasn't going to. I now understand the degree of imprecision you require." Sassy spun its wheels a little back and forth.

"Did you bury him?"

"I did not. One of the perpetrators buried him beside the other grave."

We must hurry. There is much to do. Much to learn.

Susan looked up. "Yes, there is, Voice-in-the-Walls. But I know nothing that will help me solve this puzzle yet." She began pacing the room again. Sassy followed close behind her, making little whirring noises with its wheels.

You heard what Alvion True said.

Susan whirled in place. "Yes, I heard. Where are you? I can't keep talking to air."

I am in the walls. That's where I am.

"Well, what do you look like?"

I look like nothing. I am a partition of the AI that runs this facility. Alvion True made me separate.

"Oooooh!" Susan stamped her foot in frustration. "You are not helpful. What is the problem here?"

Alvion True did not know. He attempted to discover. He was severely damaged with a projectile weapon and expired.

"There wasn't anything you could do to save him?"

Human medical intervention is not part of my programming suite.

"Well, isn't that just great." Susan threw her arms in the air. She whirled around to continue pacing and tripped over Sassy.

Susan slumped to the floor, holding her shin. "Don't follow so close." She hitched up the leg of her jeans. A trickle of blood ran down her shin.

Sassy whirred up close. "That's blood. Alvion True leaked blood. Are you going to die now?"

Sassy pulled back a little. "I don't want you to die too. You have to fix the problem."

Sassy sounded so sad and worried that Susan felt a small smile creep across her face. She patted its box top. "It's OK, Sassy. This little scrape won't kill me."

I have accessed your records: Susan Sinclair. Born in the nation known as Canada at that time. Grew to womanhood in that country. Accessed crystal at age ten. Died—

"I don't want to know!" Susan jumped to her feet. "Really, what year is this now?"

This is the year 128GE of the new reckoning.

"Wait, the year 128? Wouldn't that have been cavemen and clubs and paintings on the walls?" Susan looked around. "Am I in a cave?"

This is the year 128 after the Great Exit. Calculating. . . . In your reckoning, this would be the year 2256. Susan slumped onto Sassy's lid. "I'm in the future? I'm waaaaay in the future! Nobody told me I'd end up in the future." Susan spread her hands wide. "Why me?"

A deep dive and an unlock of sealed records show that you were present at the creation of Ma'at's five crystals. You are unique among Crystal Keepers.

"Five? Did you say 'five'?" Susan sat bolt upright. "There are four crystals," she declared.

Five.

"Four." Susan counted them off on her fingers. "North, south, east, and west."

You have omitted the blue crystal in your count.

Susan's brows furrowed. "I left two behind in the tomb." Susan tapped her finger on her chin, remembering. "They didn't snap off, so I left them. Mrs. Coleman told me there were four, so I left the other two."

The blue crystal was revealed to the world in the mid twenty-first century. I have no record of another crystal.

Susan shuddered. "Well, I'm not going back into the tomb to find it," she said.

Noted.

Susan sighed. "Right. Well, I'm here now, so I better get on with it."

She pointed at the wall and then tucked in her finger, realizing she had no idea where to point.

"Oh yes, to get back to an earlier question. Where exactly is here?"

You are currently one kilometer and forty-eight meters aft of the forward airlock and landing area. You are occupying Backup Control Room B.

"OK, but where is this control room."

Sassy made a squeaky little noise and gave a little wriggle. Its voice sounded muffled when it spoke. "I can take you and show you. That will be quickest."

Susan sprang up. "Sorry, Sassy, was I squashing you?"

Sassy whirled in place. "My wheels are still working, Susan. Come this way." Sassy headed for the wall again.

Use the walking tunnel!

"Oh yes." Sassy swerved to the right. A larger section of the wall folded open, revealing a large passage beyond.

With a sigh of relief, Susan hurried after Sassy as it sped along on the tile floor.

Finally, I might get some answers. Susan shook her head in wonder. *The future? There's so much I don't know. So many questions. But I do know there is a problem here. Two problems.*

8
There's a World in Here

The passage sloped gentle upward. Sassy sped on. Susan hurried to catch up. The only sounds she heard were her footsteps and the whir of Sassy's wheels.

Suddenly, Sassy swerved left into a small chamber let into the side of the tunnel. It stopped short in front of the far wall.

A tight beam of light shot out of one side of its box illuminating a control panel set into the wall. Sassy danced the light over the panel in a quick pattern.

Susan heard a quiet motor kick in, and the wall in front of her edged open.

Light and sound flooded in. So much all at once. Susan covered her eyes against the glare. She took a deep breath. The air smelled like a forest just after rain. She heard birds singing. Ducks, she heard ducks.

Susan stepped through the doorway and stood on a tiled path. The tiles wobbled slightly under her feet. She heard a sound from home—the whoosh of a large bird flying close. She squinted and caught a glimpse of a bald eagle on the wing. It landed on the top of a nearby tree. Susan saw its head swiveling around, king of all it surveyed.

From watching the eagle, Susan's attention was drawn to the entire scene. From where she stood, she could see across the land stretched out in front of her. Green fields ran down to a large pond, which sparkled in the light. To her left, she saw a forest growing into the distance. She saw some pine trees, but most trees were alders. A tree covered in white flowers caught her eye. It looked like a dogwood in bloom. "Sassy, this place looks like the countryside around my home. Are we in the Pacific Northwest?"

"Um, not exactly. We engineered this place to mimic the ecology of the Pacific Northwest. It's coming along nicely. Now that we have the last shipment of creatures here, we will be ready for people in a few years."

"Shipment of creatures? Is this a zoo?"

"Zoo? Checking, checking."

Susan watched a band of golden light running back and forth along one side of Sassy.

"This is not a zoo, Susan Sinclair."

"Well, tell me. What is this place? It looks like home and then it doesn't." Susan threw her hands in the air. "I can't see one building anywhere. Where are the houses?"

Sassy whirled in place. It extended its arm and waved it as Susan had. "Look up, Susan. Look up."

Susan did.

She slumped to the ground. "There's another pond up there. I can see a lake in the sky." Susan peered up. She could see land up there. As she watched, a flock of white birds flew over that lake. She watched them settle into the upside down reeds.

"Yes, welcome to New Hope." Sassy used its arm to gently take her hand.

"I don't understand. Where am I? What is this place?"

Sassy moved until it was directly in front of her.

"You are inside an asteroid. Do you know what an asteroid is?"

Susan looked out over the scene. "I'm inside a big rock in space?"

"Yes, yes, you get the idea."

"So people are out in space now?"

"Well, yes, there was the Great Exit 128 Earth years ago."

"So people live in space?"

"Well, there's many domes on the Moon and on Mars, but people also built large space stations to exploit the resources that are out here. There's

Clarion Cry, and Faint Hope, and Glory Be, and Down and Dirty. They're all space stations. But this place is something new."

"It's an asteroid, right? It was whizzing around in space. And someone came along and made it hollow?"

"Yes. I did." "I was bigger then."

Susan stood and dusted off her jeans. "I can't take any more explanations right now." She pointed at the pond. "Is it safe for me to go down there? I'd like to take a look."

"No, the men who killed Alvion True are still working in the cargo bay. I don't think you should venture out."

Susan ducked back through the doorway. "How do you know they're still here?"

"I would have heard the airlocks before they left."

Susan took a big breath. She wanted to curl up and hide. Susan imagined she could feel a bullet hitting her chest. She rubbed the spot. Then she straightened her shoulders with determination.

"I need to know what they are doing and why they killed Alvion True. How can I get close enough to hear and see what's going on?"

Sassy rocked back and forth. "Not safe. Not safe. You must not put yourself in such danger."

Susan pushed down on Sassy's lid to stop it jiggling. "Think," she ordered. "There must be some way for me to learn what they're doing and why they're doing it."

Sassy's lights began to swirl all the way around its top. "Thinking, thinking, thinking." The lights changed from a light gold to a sharper, darker amber. "Accessing, accessing."

Susan tapped her foot in frustration. "What is going on?"

"There is a storage device in the cargo bay. I am accessing it now."

Silence.

"And?" Susan twirled her fingers in a get-on-with-it motion.

Sassy whirred over to the chamber wall. There was a smoothed patch there. Sassy extruded its cord again and the screen activated.

"Aren't you done yet, Droner?" A loud, angry voice issued from the wall.

Susan heard a reply, but it was too muffled to understand. The screen was showing light, but no picture. "What's wrong with the picture?"

"Accessing, accessing." A pause. "Someone, sometime, threw a cleaning rag over this storage device. Its camera is obscured," Sassy replied.

Susan sighed with frustration. "Is there another storage device in the area?"

"Positioning, positioning."

The screen lit up. Susan could now view the cargo bay. To her, the sight was stunning.

9

The Cargo Bay

The cargo bay looked huge, bigger than two soccer fields. Susan peered at the screen in wonder.

She saw a spaceship. It rested on the floor, which looked to have enough room to house at least two more spacecraft of the same size. All spaceships looked sleek and graceful, on Susan's television. This ship looked like a monster. It was big and bulgy, antennae and sensors sprouted out all over it.

"Sassy, that's a spaceship? I thought they had to be smooth and streamlined."

Sassy waved its arm at the screen. "They only have to be aerodynamic if they are going into an atmosphere. This plodder would never set down on a planet, not even Mars. It loads in space and moves in space. The cargo is shuttled up to the ship through a planet's gravity well. This one is big and bulky, and ugly too. But it carries a lot."

The side of the craft gaped open, and a ramp led from the floor into the interior. Susan watched two men appear in the spacecraft doorway. Roughly dressed in pants with many pockets, and torn, dirty t-shirts, they started down the ramp. Between them, they wrestled a huge box. It twisted and turned on the ramp.

"Watch it! Don't let the thing fall," one man yelled. The other heaved mightily at his corner, and they managed to get the box moving smoothly down the ramp to the floor.

"What does it matter if it drops and smashes anyway?" This man mopped at his brow. His hair was sheared away from one side of his head, and Susan saw that the skin on that side of his face was puckered and looked red.

"It matters because we've still got more to move out, and it will be harder if we have to move around broken bits, stupid." The other smacked Scarface upside his head.

"Ouch, careful."

"Always getting into fights, you. You're lucky the laser only got half your face." The bigger man clouted him again. He jerked his head toward the ramp. "C'mon, lots more cages to go. We're behind. I want to get out of here. This place gives me the creeps."

They moved up the ramp and into the ship.

Susan took notice of the boxes strewn across the deck. She guessed there were about sixty scattered around. There was no order to their arrangement. It looked as though they were pushed off all over the place.

"Are these the animal deliveries Alvion talked about?"

"Yes." Sassy spun in a small circle. "They are not supposed to be like that. They need to be moved out into the biosphere. These men need to get them moving."

Susan shook her head. "They don't look like caring-for-animals types. I don't think they're going to do anything more than they absolutely have to."

"Watch it, you clumsy goat. Pull you weight." The bossy one was yelling again.

Another cage emerged.

"Nah." Scarface kicked the cage, and it rolled down the ramp across the floor and slammed into another cage. Both men laughed.

No sound came from the cages.

"Are the animals alright?" Susan asked.

"Should be. They're in a deep sleep for the trip. The project leaders, Sirrahs Agate, Heath and Shale, would take every care on Earth to package them safely for the journey."

The men walked over to a couple of low cages and sat to rest.

"How much do you think they paid for this lot?" Scarface asked.

"More than you'll ever see," Bossy answered. "They're so rich in the domes they can build a place like this. Out here. Just so they never have to touch Earth with their fancy shoes. What do they care what it cost? They'll just charge us more for what we need from them."

"Oooh, listen to you. Sirrah thinks he knows politics. Why don't you move out there if you don't like the way it is?"

Bossy shrugged. "I was on Down and Dirty for a while. Too many rules. Went back to Earth for my downtime and never left again. Except for gigs like this. I still space when I can get jobs that suit me

Scarface scratched at the cage he sat on. "There must be someone out here who would pay for these animals on the quiet. Let's load them up, find a buyer, and live like the rich do."

Bossy punched him in the arm. "Always the idiot, you. Where you going to keep 'em so they'll live? Took 'em over twenty years to prepare this place with all the accelerated technology they could muster. How you going to hide 'em? How you going to feed 'em? How would you and I survive the next month when our 'contractor' on Earth found out what we'd done?" He used air quotes around the word contractor. "And they would find out." Bossy scowled and folded his arms over his chest.

Scarface shrugged and kicked the side of the cage.

"Hey, Droner, any progress over there?" Bossy turned his head toward the far wall away from the ramp. This drew Susan's attention to another man, standing at a small screen in the corner.

"Um, still downloading the revised sequence into the AI," Droner answered. "And my name is Humphrey."

"Haw, what sort of a name is that?" Bossy slapped his leg and hooted.

"An old and honorable one," Humphrey snarled in reply.

"Well, you'd be finished by now, if you hadn't insisted on burying the nosy guy."

Humphrey turned and scowled at Bossy. "The program was downloading. I was waiting. So I buried the dead man next to the other grave I found. These are wild animals, and once released, they would have eaten his body."

Bossy arm butted Scarface. "Sirrah thinks he's better than us." Then he turned and shouted to Humphrey. "What makes you think we're gonna go to all the work of hauling these cages out into the trees, Droner? Hurry up. We can't leave until you finish what you're up to over there."

Humphrey turned his attention back to the screen. "It takes as long as it takes." He sniffed. "We're fifty percent infiltrated."

Susan could hardly believe what she was hearing. Animals were priceless, and they were being treated so carelessly. And what about the man in the corner, Humphrey, infiltrating the AI. That didn't sound good. Susan knew these were the villains, but how could she stop them?

Susan turned to Sassy. "What will happen to all those cages and the animals if they're just left there?"

Sassy jigged in place. "When they open the airlock to space, the animals will all die from decompression and lack of oxygen."

"What can we do, Sassy? We can't let that happen."

"The information AI received was that each cage has a set of wheels like mine. They all link together and can be pulled through the main doors and into the biosphere."

"So can we do that?"

"Not in the time that it will take them to prepare for space and open the airlock doors."

"Then we must start sooner. Can the storage devices link the cages and pull them down the path you're talking about?"

Sassy jigged some more. "Not in time, not in time. There are not enough of us. No time, no time."

"Then we need the airlock door not to open until we're ready. Do you think Partition can get the AI to keep the doors closed?"

Sassy stopped jigging. "I'll ask." Another cord extruded from it into a different port on the wall. "Accessing, accessing."

10

The Bosses Called

Susan fidgeted from foot to foot. It would be awful if all those animals died. In this future, they seemed to be even more valuable than they were in her era. A lot of time and effort and money had gone into building this place for them. Over twenty years to build. That would explain the size of the trees she had seen.

Susan stared at the screen. Bossy and Scarface, hauled cages big and small out of their spaceship and dumped them around the cargo bay.

Susan pinched her arm. Ouch. She wasn't dreaming. She really was looking at a spaceship, pulled into the cargo bay of a hollowed-out asteroid that was growing a forest and ponds around the inner surfaces. She shook her head in wonder.

Sassy nudged up against Susan's leg. "Partition is having trouble gaining control of the airlock doors," it said.

Brrrring. Susan looked around. It sounded like an old telephone. Brrrring. The sound came again.

Sassy wasn't reacting. Susan glanced at the screen. Bossy and Scarface were resting again. They hadn't noticed the sound either.

Wooooooowooooooowoooooo. Bossy and Scarface leaped to their feet. Bossy grabbed at his pocket, and Scarface gestured at his forehead like a half salute. The wailing sound continued, getting louder and louder. Scarface began to tremble. Susan watched him run his finger around the collar of his t-shirt, like he was suddenly too hot.

Bossy pulled a small device from his pocket. He held it up and turned until he found a screen on the wall. He pointed his device, pushed a button, and an image sprang into being. A man and a woman, sprawled on an opulent couch, staring straight a-head. The woman lifted a crystal glass to her painted lips. She sipped delicately at the contents. She reached forward and put the glass on the beautiful, polished wooden table in front of them.

"CONNECTION ESTABLISHED, DARLINGS," a computer voice cooed.

The two kissed briefly, then turned their attention to the screen. "I told you, Begonia. I told you that archaic phone ring wouldn't get their attention." The woman shrugged her fur collar up closer around her throat.

"Well, your siren certainly did the trick, Grenville, dear." She gestured at the screen. "Can we get on with the business now?" She smiled sweetly out at the two standing in the cargo bay.

Then her smile changed into an angry scowl. "I see you've only half done the job you are being paid too handsomely for."

Grenville sat forward. He peered through the screen. "I can see what you mean, darling." He patted Begonia's knee. Then he scowled back at the screen. "Get those cages linked and out into the biosphere," he snarled.

Bossy shrugged. He hunched his shoulders and hung his head. "But, Boss, what difference does it make where they are? They'll be gone just like everything else."

There was a delay as Susan watched. *I suppose it takes time for the transmission to go from space to wherever they are—even in the future.*

Then the video started up again.

Begonia chuckled. "You hired them, darling." She waved her hand dismissively. "You explain it to them."

Grenville snarled. "Now you listen, you over-priced space jockeys, without proof that the cages are in the biosphere, we don't get our final payment. We have that two billion bits ear-marked for extensions to this little house of ours. We have expenses, you know."

"And," Begonia held up a finger, "can you imagine what would happen to you and your families if we don't get that payment?" She pointed a black painted fingernail at the screen and shook her head. "You don't even want to think about that."

Grenville nodded in agreement. "It won't be pretty." He pointed at the screen. "Now get those cages moving. Get them out of the cargo bay, and out into the grounds." He waved his hand around. "The contract specified Island Pond."

Begonia nodded in agreement. "And get lots of really good visuals. We need proof, and it will be nice to have a memento for our collection."

The two laughed together and hugged each other. It was not a nice laugh.

"Um," Bossy nodded and bounced on his toes, "um, do we open the cages too?" They waited through the delay.

Grenville sprang to his feet. "Dolt," he yelled. "Stupid!"

Begonia shook her head and scowled. "They'd probably let the wolves out first so that they could be waiting at the cage doors when they release the deer."

Humphrey walked over to join the other two. "The AI is programmed for controlled releases in the correct order." He smirked at Bossy and Scarface, then turned toward the screen and waited.

Grenville slumped back onto the couch and rested his feet on an ottoman. "Why, hello Humphrey, how is your end of our little project going?"

Humphrey turned to the other two. He grabbed the little device from Bossy. “Get moving on those cages. We don’t want to be here any longer than necessary.” He turned back to the screen. “We’re almost ready, Sirrahs,” he said, with a deferential bow.

Again the wait.

“Good.” Both nodded, with pleased looks on their faces.

“How much delay have you set up?” Begonia asked.

Grenville answered. “I asked for fourteen days.”

Begonia frowned. “Will that give us time to receive our money and hide it in our system so it’s untouchable? We wouldn’t want to pay any taxes or anything.”

Grenville rubbed his hands together. “Should be adequate, my dear. The Consortium will be confused for a start and wonder what’s gone wrong. It will take them a while to figure out they can’t fix the problem remotely, and by then, it will be way, way too late.”

The two cackled laughter, and Humphrey joined in.

“I do so love it when everything works out just perfectly.” Begonia stroked her fur collar.

“Yes, just that Marvin fellow out there. That’s a loose end we’ll have to fix permanently.”

“Oh, you’re so clever. I forgot about little Marvin. Such a small amount of money we paid him to give us the contract so we could charge the Consortium trillions to create the biosphere. Did the dolt really think we would allow such competition for our own resort to survive?” Begonia peered at her nails. “Yes, he will have to go.” She sighed. “More expense.”

Grenville nodded with a smirk and turned to the screen. “We’ll see you when you return.” Grenville leaned forward. “Out now.”

The faces disappeared from the screen, replaced by a shimmering logo.

Susan squinted to make it out.

The logo faded to black. Susan slumped to the tiles. She wanted to brush herself all over to get rid of the feel of those people. But she still watched.

Humphrey walked over to return the device to Bossy. “Hey, Droner, you didn’t mention the extra guy that showed up,” Bossy said

“Wasn’t necessary,” Humphrey answered. “You dealt with it, and I cleaned up your mess. End of story.”

Bossy leaned on the cage. “Sure would like to know where he came from, though, and how he got here.”

Scarface shrugged. “Too late now. His DigiD said he was from Clarion’s Cry.”

Humphrey shrugged. “Well, he’s gone now.” Humphrey turned and sauntered back to the console where he continued checking the readouts. Susan gasped when she saw Humphrey pull a cable out of his shoulder and plug himself into the wall.

Susan shuddered and turned away. She focused on the other two.

“Come on. Let’s get this cage train moving.” Bossy and Scarface started pushing the cages into place and hooking them together.

“Sooner we can get away from here, the better I’ll like it.” Scarface shuddered. “The air doesn’t smell. The dirt’s not covered up. There’s birds out there. They could poop on your head flying around like that.”

“Yeah,” Bossy agreed. “And the trees they’re really tall. What if one fell on you.”

Scarface frowned. “I hadn’t thought of that.”

Bossy sighed. “Come on. Let’s get it over with.”

Susan sighed. She knew more, but now she had more questions. *At least I know some of the things to ask now. And I know there is definitely a problem. I’ve got less than fourteen days to fix it. And I’ll remember the name Sutton too. That’s easy.*

11

More about Sassy

Sassy pulled its connector out of the wall and retracted it into a compartment. Susan gave a quiet shudder. Then she shrugged. Somehow, with a robot, it wasn't so icky.

Susan smiled. "Well, at least their bosses have ordered them to move the cages out to the pond area. It won't matter about the airlock doors now." She turned to Sassy. "I didn't understand about them taking pictures for proof that the animals are here or the bosses don't get paid by the Cons...Consor... something like that.."

“Ah, yes, the Consortium.” Sassy blinked its lights.

“What’s a consortium?” Susan asked.

“A consortium is a group of people who get together to create a project that is too big and expensive for any one person or company to tackle. They pool their resources so that the project gets done, and then they all benefit.” Sassy’s lights showed steady white.

Susan nodded. “So this was too expensive and big for any one company . . . so a bunch of them got together to make it happen?”

Sassy bounced in place. “You’ve got it, Susan. They call themselves the Consortium of Planets and Space Stations. The CPSS. You see the letters around some places.”

Sassy turned to view the screen. “I’m pulling the cages out into the biosphere!” it exclaimed.

Susan hesitated. “What do you mean, you’re pulling the cages out?”

“Oh, that’s me out there.”

“No, Sassy, you’re here.”

“Yes, Susan, I am, but I’m also out there, pulling the cages.” Sassy waved its arm out into the biosphere. “And I’m also over there, monitoring water quality in the pond.” It waved to the right. “And back there, checking my rocket assembly. Oh, and I’m also doing dust elimination in Tunnels Sixteen, Thirty-two and Twelve at the moment.”

Susan sat cross-legged on the path. She looked at the country below her and above her, watching for signs of the cage train. “Explain how you can be in so many places please. It makes no sense.”

Sassy whirred up next to her. “Simple really,” it said. “Once the Consortium selected the asteroid they wanted for this place, they dropped off four of us. Oh, I was big then. First, we pushed the asteroid out of its usual path and into the desired orbit. Next, we deployed our communication laser systems and sensing devices on the exterior.

“There was an unfortunate occurrence at that time. Leviathan Two was made unstable by a roving piece of space junk, which rendered it vulnerable to cosmic radiation. We had to sequester it.

“The rest of us continued on. We began the hollowing out process. This asteroid is tube shaped, with pointy ends. We started at one end, and once we had the interior hollowed out to the desirable size, we calved off our propulsion rockets, which we attached to the entry point. Now the asteroid was move-able, should that be required. Then we hollowed out the interior and clustered the rock and other material in close orbit. We will eventually use it to build accommodations.

“In the bow, we formed up the landing area and cargo bay you saw. With all the large work done, we broke ourselves down even smaller. We extruded tunnelers to create the administration areas within the asteroid walls. Crawlers covered every millimeter of the surfaces to ensure no fissures had been left undiscovered or created. Then we fitted the airlock doors. The outer doors are from Leviathan One. Just because it was number one, it always thought it was the boss. Leviathan Four is the inner airlock doors. It has them open now because the cage train is still moving through. I was designated Leviathan Three."

Susan nodded. "Well, where are your doors, Sassy?"

"Oh, my doors are aft. They cover access to the propulsion units."

"So if you broke up and changed as needed, just how many pieces of you are there in here?"

"Hmm, I've never thought about it. Checking." Sassy's golden lights whizzed around its top. It made a popping sound, then said, "Counting sensors and cleaners, I'm in two thousand, four hundred and sixty-three pieces."

"Goodness. Are you in contact with them all?"

"No, some report directly to AI."

"And this happened to all three of you that are left?"

"Yes, we're everywhere, doing everything."

"Well, what about this part of you? What do you do?"

"I'm a storage device, Susan."

"Yes, but you're more than that. I know you are. You help me."

"Yes, AI saw Alvion True as an intruder. He was not scheduled to be here, so Sirrah Alvion upgraded me to semi stealth and gave me other capabilities, one of which was to keep him cloaked from AI. That's why I plug into the wall rather than communicate wirelessly. It makes my communications secure from AI. Then Alvion was killed. So when you arrived, Partition and I cloaked you. We still cloak you. I have been tasked with keeping you safe and informed, as needed."

"That's a lot to ask of a storage device, Sassy."

"Yes, but I am up to the task." It's lights glowed sky blue.

"That Humphrey guy, he had a cord in his neck. He plugged in to a wall in the corner of the cargo bay. Was he communicating with Partition too?"

Sassy went still. "No, not Partition. He must have been communicating at a deep dive level with AI."

Sassy sat for a moment. A low ping sounded. Sassy jigged once in place. "Ah, I set my reminder. I calculate four hours, twenty-six minutes, and thirty-eight seconds have elapsed since last you ate."

Susan thought about it. Her tummy rumbled. She nodded.

Sassy jigged once again in place. Susan felt a wave of heat flow out from it. Then the delicious aroma of food wafted across to her.

"I have heated risotto al funghi porcini for you."

Susan took a deep breath. Mushrooms. She lifted Sassy's lid and reached for the bowl nestled there. She pulled her hand back just before she touched it. "Hot," she said.

A little door on Sassy's side sprang open. Susan reached down and pulled out a cloth. She unwound it to find a fork and spoon. She used the corner to pick up the steaming bowl.

Carefully, she peeled back the lid, and there was lunch. Rice, mushrooms, some green stuff. It smelled wonderful.

"Thank you, Sassy. This is great."

Susan began to eat. The scrape of her fork on the bowl blended with the sounds of birds in the forest. A soft breeze gently stirred the trees. Somewhere she heard the chirring of a squirrel.

12

Heard Among the Vegetables

Susan scraped up the last grain of rice from her bowl."That was delicious." She looked around and waved the bowl about. "Where do I put this?"

"Ah." Sassy turned to the side and a small flap flew open. "I have a recycle slot. Pop it in."

Susan did so. "Wow, you've got a little door for everything. What else have you got in you?"

Sassy waved its articulated arm dismissively. "Erm, there are a few things. I resupply as needed."

It turned to the left. "Ah, here I come. I'm through the airlock doors now."

Susan peered into the distance. "I can't see you."

A screen lit up on Sassy's side. "Accessing one of my nest cams to monitor progress. Watch."

Susan moved in close and peered at the little screen.

"You're traveling on a shiny black path like the one here."

"Yes, all the paths make movement easier for most devices. They harvest kinetic energy from our passage. Travel on the paths protects the trees and undergrowth from damage also."

"It looks like the train is traveling beside a vegetable garden."

"I am. The people who will eventually live here will need to eat, and it's better if they have a ready supply on hand, so the engineer and botanist are testing out the best varieties to grow in this created climate."

Susan touched the screen in wonder. "You've thought of everything."

"Our architects did," Sassy agreed. "This is the first one they've made, so there were some mistakes. But they've had twenty-eight years to work out the details."

Susan watched as the train of cages began to wend its way through the forest.

Sassy jigged and spun. "Wait, wait. Not right. Not right. Checking, checking."

"What's happening?" Susan leaped to her feet.

Sassy didn't answer. Golden lights mixed with red zipped around. Susan had never seen them flash red before. It rushed to the wall and whipped out its cable.

"Accessing Partition. Accessing Partition. Correlate count."

You are correct device called Sassy. Eighty-seven cages were ordered, and the deposit was paid. Your count is accurate there are ninety-one cages in the train. Account for the extra four.

Sassy jigged in place. "I cannot. I will watch."

Susan had been following the conversation. She shrugged. "Maybe they had four extra animals and decided to send them along too."

"Knowing the character of the Sutton Range Resort that would be extremely unlikely," Sassy answered. "We will watch."

Susan glanced at the screen again. Sassy had switched to a lower camera, which moved to follow the cage train. Bossy and Scarface both chewed on apples. The looks on their faces were of pure pleasure and delight.

"They look happy," Susan remarked.

"They've probably never eaten a fresh apple before." Sassy observed. "They're not ripe yet, but they wouldn't know that."

Susan startled back from the view on the screen. The train was proceeding along the path, and a grave came into view. The dirt on it looked freshly turned. A few stones were pressed into the top of it. A small plastic card was hanging on a stick at one end. *I guess that's where Alvion True is*

But then next to it, another grave appeared. Grass grew among the stones spread across the top. A small cross made from tied sticks stood a little crookedly at one end. "Two graves," Susan exclaimed. "Who else was killed?"

"Her name was Spruce. It's an older grave."

"What happened to Spruce?"

"She was one of the biologists who set up this ecosystem. She coughed and coughed. She and Heath were responsible for settling the animals into the marshes and wet areas that were here then. Spruce's husband, Shale, is a forester, and he checked all the trees and vegetation.

"Spruce had the coughing sickness. In the end, it became too much for her. One day, she was cruising the wetland looking for the beaver lodge when she fell to her knees, coughing. She couldn't rise. By the time Heath and Shale reached her, she was dying. They were so sad. But Spruce said—AI heard her—she said that she would rather die in this lovely place than back on Earth, with all that choking dust and smoke, with the forests dying and the dragging burden of debt.

"Her only regret, she said, was that she wouldn't get to say goodbye to her children who were back on Earth." All Sassy's lights dimmed. "It was a very sad time."

Susan patted Sassy's top in sympathy.

Sassy's lights sprang into brightness again. "Thank you, Susan."

Susan sat thinking for a moment. "Then these aren't the only creatures to be delivered."

"You're right," Sassy agreed. "The first delivery went to the furthest end of New Hope. That one contained the insects and bees as well as the first mammals and fish." Sassy waved its arm to the right. "The next delivery stocked the center. And now, this delivery is the closest to the airlock, and is the final delivery."

<u>Watch those men. Watch them. I don't like them tromping around the biosphere unwatched. Be on guard.</u>

Sassy shook himself. "Erm, certainly, Partition. We're on it."

Susan watched its lights spin round and round, going faster and faster. For a moment, they dimmed and then flashed red, red, red.

"They're in the produce garden. They've dropped the cages by the pond and have driven me back to the garden. They're looting the produce garden!"

Susan peered at Sassy's little screen. Yes, she could see the two men pulling plants out of the ground. Scarface removed his shirt and threw carrots, potatoes, and beets onto it until it wouldn't hold any more. Bossy found a box and attacked the apple tree. Green or ripe, he didn't care. He stripped the tree of every fruit he could reach.

Then Sassy accessed an audio feed.

Bossy pointed to a row of tomato plants. "Get those," he ordered Scarface. Instead of picking off the fruit, Scarface just hauled the plants out and clutched as many of them as he could in his arms.

Bossy shook his head and moved to the peach tree. Here, the fruit was ripe. Bossy began picking them and tossing them into his box. "Do you realize this is the food that only extremely rich people get to eat?"

He paused to shake his fist in the direction of the cargo bay. "Take that, lovey-dovey Sirrahs. We'll be eating as good as you on the way home to the Mud Wallow." They laughed.

"But won't they know we've taken all this stuff?" Scarface asked.

Bossy shrugged. "How will they know? Didn't Droner say there was only a couple of weeks left? Couple of weeks, and this place is history. His-tor-y."

Bossy threw an overripe peach at Scarface, who grabbed the nearest one off the tree and threw it at Bossy. Laughing and screaming, the two started a food fight.

Sassy's lights dimmed. "What a waste."

Susan turned to Sassy. "What do you think he meant when he said there was only a couple of weeks left?"

Sassy's lights blinked. "I didn't understand that."

Susan thought a moment. "That other guy, the one they called Humphrey, he was over in the corner and it looked like he was working on a computer there."

"He talked about the time too." Sassy jigged in place.

"I bet he did something to AI. Something that is going to harm this place. I bet that's what I'm here to fix." Susan sat with a groan. "That's just great. I need help downloading a song in my time. What could I possibly know about computers here and now?"

Warning. Danger. Intruders in the produce garden, Partition shouted.

Then thunderous music started up, loud and rousing.

Leave the garden immediately. Partition's voice was even louder than the music.

Out now! Mooooove it.

The music swelled even louder.

Susan covered her ears.

Bossy and Scarface froze in fright. Then they picked up their burdens and scurried up the path, panting and running, stumbling and gasping. But in all that hurried rush, they carefully held their precious stolen fruit and vegetables. As soon as the airlock doors closed behind them, the music cut off. Sassy hurried to plug in again.

They were spoiling my vegetables. I had experiments in place in those beds.

"Well done, Partition. You drove them off."

Humph, somebody had to.

"What was that music you played, Partition? I recognize it, but I don't know what it's called."

That, Susan of old, is popularly called "The Ride of the Valkyries," composed by Richard Wagner. First performed in 1876 at the—

"Yes, ok," Susan said. "We have a problem. We think those men interfered with the AI in some way. We think they have set this facility up to destroy itself."

Impossible. The AI and I have the most sophisticated fail-safes possible. Nobody can beam in any sort of control that would disrupt our smooth function.

Susan put her hands on her hips and glared at the screen. "In my time, people are always saying things like that, and then a couple of months later, they admit they've lost millions of files containing people's personal information."

That was then, Susan. We are much more powerful now and can detect and remove all unwanted intrusions beamed at us.

Susan turned to Sassy. "Did you record any of what we saw in the airlock and what they said in the garden?"

Sassy rocked on its little wheels. "No, Susan. You didn't ask me to."

"Right." Susan huffed out a breath. "Then I suggest you tell Partition exactly everything we saw and heard."

"Complying." Sassy's lights glowed green and then began to rhythmically slide around its top.

Susan looked out over the forest scene. There were the cages—ninety-one when there should only be eighty-seven. Susan peered down at them and began counting. Some of the smaller ones were piled on top of larger ones. There was no way to get a reliable count.

"Sassy, I'm going down to check out the cages," she announced.

"What if the men return?" Sassy responded in a slow voice. Obviously, most of its attention was focused on Partition.

Susan shrugged. "Then I'll hide in the forest," she said and marched down the slope toward the cages, which were standing beside the pond.

13

The Cages

As Susan walked down the slope, the sounds of the forest enveloped her. She heard the ducks again. The leaves rustled softly in the breeze, almost like a welcome. She only realized there were frogs when they stopped their croaking as she neared the pond.

There stood the cages. The men hadn't even unhooked them from each other. Susan wandered along the line. She ran her fingers across the cages as she went.

A small cage on top of a larger one caught her attention. It was at about her eye level. It was formed from fibers all squashed together. Not wood, but like the particleboard her father had used to build a few shelves in her mother's studio. There were no bars; it was more like a box than a cage. A label flapping in the breeze caught her eye. "*Eutamias minimus*," Susan read. She frowned. *What was that?* She flipped the label and found a picture of a chipmunk. *Ah*.

Next to the label, she noticed a little spy hole. Susan put her eye up close. She saw only darkness. Her fingers found a little button beside the hole. She pressed and soft light showed her the inside of the box. Three little chipmunks lay curled together on a soft cloth. They were fast asleep. They looked relaxed, chubby, and comfortable.

What else is here? Susan moved along the line.

A large cage stood next, it looked much stronger and made of something smooth and almost plastic looking. The label read, *Ursus americanus—Black bear*. Only one in there. A medium cage, cougar. Susan peered in—*asleep*. She didn't want to be around when that cage door opened.

Coyotes, deer, elk, mink, striped skunk. Most of the animals from the Pacific Northwest were represented. Susan wondered how one or two of each animal was going to be enough to keep the biosphere running smoothly.

Then Susan found a cage that was different. It was large and made of the plastic looking material, but this one had no label. No spy hole. What was in this one? *Maybe this is the Sasquatch*. Susan laughed to herself.

Maybe not a Sasquatch, but certainly a mystery. *Was this one of the extra four?* Susan searched along the line. Yes, there were exactly four cages with this shape, no spy hole and no label.

Well, it will be interesting to see what emerges. She thought, with a grin. *But I don't think I want to be standing too close to greet whatever comes out.*

Susan hurried back up the slope to tell Sassy of her findings.

14

Some Cages Open

Susan assumed that Sassy was still busy communicating with Partition. The robot hadn't moved, and its green lights rotated as before.

She sat on a rock and looked out at the scene around her. So different. And yet, also the same. The trees and clearings looked like the ones she and Judy rode their bikes through. But at home, there was sky above, not more ponds and trees. She sighed and let her mind rest. *I'm in the future. It's still hard to believe.*

The men had called Earth "the Mud Wallow." *Maybe pollution and warming just went on and on. Maybe people didn't begin to fix the problems. Partition had mentioned something that sounded scary. The GE.* Susan wracked her brains for what it had meant. *GE, yes, the Great Exit. What had happened? Did the population have to get away from Earth? People in my time talked about going into space . . . colonizing Mars . . . maybe that was it. Susan rested her chin in her hands. There's so much I don't know. How can I help? A Crystal Guardian was killed. I'm not a detective. I'm sure the problem is to do with those horrible people on the screen and what the droner guy was doing in the back corner of the cargo bay.*

Sassy's connector cable slapped back into its niche. Susan heard the whir of its wheels.

"The airlock is now open, and the ship is departing."

Susan jolted out of her thoughts, "They're getting away?"

"You were not safe while they remained. They had the correct codes. AI released them."

"What will happen now?"

"We're not sure. Partition is having difficulty channeling AI. There is some sort of glitch in the system."

"I think that Humphrey guy was tampering with AI while the others handled the cages."

Sassy rocked back and forth on its wheels. "Possible. Possible."

<Phase One sleep reversal. Initiating. Now.>

Susan jumped to her feet. "Who was that?" She looked around wildly.

Sassy made a chuckling noise. It sounded like a tin whistle blowing the scales quickly up and down. "That was AI." Sassy moved to the edge of the path and looked down at the clearing where the cages sat. "The first lot of creatures will start to awaken."

Susan pointed out the four different cages.

Doors began to pop open, not all though.

"Why are some opening and not others?"

"The programming lets the animals that are prey out first. They need to run and hide and be fully aware before we release the predators. The hunters will sleep for a few more days."

Susan leaned forward in excitement. "Sassy, the four extra cages are open."

"You are correct, Susan. This is most irregular. The ecological balance is carefully worked out here. I must inform Partition of this problem." Sassy whirled on the spot and hurried back to the wall jack. Its light display flashed as it went.

Susan settled down to watch what would emerge. What creature could have been slipped into the mix? Susan thought back to the Suttons. They didn't act like people who would send extra creatures for the goodwill.

Movement caught Susan's attention. Yes, one of the small cages sitting on top of a larger one had jiggled. A head peeped out. Susan watched as a tiny nose lifted and sniffed the air. First one foot, then another emerged. Cautiously an otter stepped out into the light. Susan sighed. The creature looked so beautiful stretching its back and looking around. It twirled in a circle, getting its bearings, then leaped from the top of the large cage and scampered into the reeds beside the pond.

Small creatures emerged along the line of cages. They paused, shook themselves, and ran off into the surrounding trees. A deer stood beside her cage and used the edge to give herself a good back rub. She used her back leg to reach a tricky part on her side and then trotted off into the forest, without looking back.

Susan ran her eye along the line of cages. She gasped. She leaned forward and squinted to see if that changed what she saw. Standing beside one of the four extra cages stood a boy. A boy!

He stretched his arms up high and gave a huge jaw-cracking yawn. Then he scratched at his hair, which was tangled all over his head. It hung down into his eyes. The boy worked his shoulders as though to get kinks out, then strolled along the line of cages.

He stopped at the next unusual one. He tapped his knuckles on the roof. Susan chuckled. *It's like he's knocking on the door*. A head poked out. This person looked around at the scenery, nodded to the first boy and pulled back into his cage.

First Boy shrugged and moved on to the next unusual cage. This time, when he rapped, a girl emerged. She was almost as tall as the boy. She immediately wrapped her arms around him, and they hugged and laughed. They stood back and looked at each other and, still laughing, reached out to ruffle each other's hair.

They look very pleased with themselves, Susan thought.

Susan saw First Boy ask a question. In answer, the girl turned and waved her arm further down the line of cages. There, a younger girl stood on top of her cage. She was staring intently into the surrounding forest. The other two called out to her, and she immediately jumped down and ran to them. They hugged and laughed together. The new girl pointed off toward the pond and immediately set off in that direction. First Boy caught her coat and pulled her back. He shook his head at her. She put her hands on her hips and frowned.

The three looked back toward the other cage. That boy now sat on the roof and stared intently into the distance. Elbowing each other, the three walked back to where he sat.

The older girl tapped his arm, and the boy jumped. He turned slowly to face the three children. Between them, they hauled him down for a group hug. Then the four of them moved off a little from the cages. They sat in a circle. It looked as though they had a lot to discuss.

Susan hurried into the tunnel. She had to tell Sassy.

15

Children!

"Children!"

Sassy whirred around in a tight circle. "Children! This is not allowed. Humans are not scheduled for another five Earth years. The animals need time to truly integrate into the ecosystem."

Susan shrugged. "Well, whatever, there are four children sitting in a circle down by the cages. I saw them. They're there." She jerked her head. "Come and look if you don't believe me."

Instead Sassy rushed back to the wall. Out flew its cable, and it was soon busy with Partition again.

Susan noticed that she was beginning to understand Sassy's lights. The speed they traveled around its perimeter indicated what was going on in its head —if it had a head. When they first noticed four extra cages, the lights flashed. The color of the lights also meant something, she decided.

Susan checked on Sassy. It was still standing motionless beside the wall.

She decided to go check on the children.

***

Things had changed during her absence. Their cages were pulled out of the line and gathered into a circle. All the openings faced inwards. A stretch of canvas formed a roof over the center. The children had built themselves a secure cubby house.

Sassy whirred up beside her. "It is dusk now, Susan. Soon it will be night. You must come into the tunnels. We have opened the biologist's accommodation for you."

Susan stood and smoothed down her sweatshirt. "Will they be safe?"

"There are no predators about yet. They look well entrenched there. AI will be informed and will have decided on their disposition by the time it is light again."

Susan yawned and stretched. "Well, if they're safe. I am tired. Let's go."

She walked through the tunnels beside Sassy, but her mind was out in the forest with four children. They didn't act surprised to find themselves in this place. *What made them come here? How did they stowaway on that ship and survive the trip from Earth?* So many questions. Susan yawned again.

She hardly looked at the room Sassy brought her to. All she saw was the bed. Narrow, but with sheets and a pillow. The duvet had a picture of a hummingbird on it. It was soft as she pulled it up around her shoulders. Sassy dimmed the lights. Susan shut her eyes.

***

Susan opened her eyes.

Sassy stood right beside her bed.

She sat up startled. She looked around. Then her circumstances all came flooding back to her. She flopped back onto the pillow.

"Is it morning already?"

Sassy bounced in place. "Breakfast will be scrambled eggs, with English muffins and bacon strips."

Susan threw back the covers. "Can I have a shower or something first?"

"The fold leads to an ablution area."

Susan jumped up. Moving had made her realize just how much she needed a washroom. She rushed to the fold. It opened. The tunnel. She looked around.

"Ahem," Sassy waved its articulated arm. "The other fold."

Susan turned and walked through the 'other fold'. "It should have a sign on it," she muttered.

***

The smell of bacon drew Susan back into the sleeping room. Sassy stood by a small table hinged out from the wall. With her hair still damp, but her body "blown dry," Susan lifted Sassy's lid. She took a deep breath. Breakfast.

Sassy extruded a napkin, and Susan lifted out her plate.

"Did you find everything you needed, Susan?" Sassy asked. It used its articulated arm to place flatware on the table.

"Yes." Susan nodded. "I was surprised at how much water I could have for my shower though."

"How so?"

"My cousin Jason told me that in Australia where he lives, they have timers in the shower so that people don't use too much water. Water is precious and must be saved." Susan shrugged. "I hurried because I thought it would be the same here."

Sassy bounced on his wheels. "Ah, all water is recycled through the ecosystem here. The ponds and lakes are designed to clean the water for continued use."

"Was the water always here?" she asked between forkfuls of egg.

"Some of the outer asteroids are made of almost entirely water. We grabbed one once we had the hollow at optimum size," Sassy answered. "It rained continually for two years, three months and fourteen days, in your time reckoning."

"Then what happened?"

"The water gradually settled into the natural deep places, and we landscaped it further to make the ponds. There are also hidden cisterns supplying taps and sewerage systems." Sassy's arm stretched out and delicately picked up a piece of egg, which had fallen off Susan's fork. It tucked it into its recycle compartment.

"New Hope is designed to accommodate over three thousand people when it is fully matured."

It continued with its lecture. "Your shower, and the four new children, will not tax the system. Partition ran the numbers last night, and we will have to adjust point zero zero one percent for the added call on resources. This is quite within acceptable limits for this moment in the maturation of the system."

Susan sighed. "I suppose you mean that everything is going to be alright, and the children and I aren't going to wreck the whole place."

"That's what I said." Sassy bounced its wheels.

Susan scraped her plate clean.

"What about the children?" she asked, placing her used plate into the recycle compartment. "Have you checked on them?"

"We swiveled one of my pond monitoring cameras so that it took in their camp. Nothing disturbed them during the night."

Susan scraped some crumbs off the table. "I wonder what they're having for breakfast."

She stood and stretched. "I suppose I better go down there and meet them."

Sassy started for the door. "You will be safe. AI is accessing Earth records. It's important to know who these children are, why they came, and how they got on that ship."

Susan followed Sassy closely. She had no idea where she was in the tunnel complex.

I need some chalk to draw on the walls so that I can find my way around. The crystals in her pocket jabbed her leg. *Or I could just jump to that room, if I need to.*

16

Making Friends?

When Susan stepped out of the tunnels. She took a moment to enjoy the fresh air. Deep breaths drew the crisp air deep into her lungs. From her lookout, she saw no movement at the children's camp, so Susan decided to walk around the pond rather than walk directly down to meet them.

The trees she walked through were not as big as the trees around her house at home, but she saw cedars and firs among the alders growing along her way. A few shrubs grew under the trees; she saw Oregon grape and salal. In a small clearing where the light shone down to the forest floor, Susan saw ocean spray. She recognized the plant because it was thick with fluffy white flowers. Susan paused and pushed her nose into the hanging fluff. It smelled like home.

When she reached the edge of the pond, she pushed through reeds growing at the edge so that she could look out across the water. Her movements startled a family of ducks foraging in the shallows. They took off squawking. They settled on an island in the middle of the pond. She could hear them quacking angrily in the reeds.

Honking drew her attention to the right, and she watched as a vee of geese swept down, landing in the water. Several paddled over to the bank and stepped onto land, with much wagging of tails and flapping of wings.

Susan settled on the grass to watch. It all looked familiar—but not. A loud splash drew her attention. Another splash followed, and Susan heard laughter. She jumped up to see what was happening.

The children were frolicking in the water. Laughing and splashing, they played together.

Ah, they're up. Time to get on with it.

"Hello," Susan called and waved.

"Hello," she called again, louder.

The children went instantly silent. They crouched, looking around. The bigger boy pointed at her. And then they all hurried from the water, gathered up their clothes and disappeared into the trees.

Susan sighed. It was like her first time at Karate class. Everyone else knew each other, and she had to find a way into the group.

These children acted as though they were afraid . . . of her.

Susan decided to give them a little time to settle. They had seen her. Let them think about that for a while.

She lay back in the grass. The day was beginning to warm, and the smells and sounds soothed. It had been a jangling time for her.

She pulled the crystals from her pocket. The two were still stuck together. Hers showed lights within as she peered into the depths. The blue crystal had just the tiniest little spark, way within. “The Crystal of the Outer Regions,” Alvion had called it. There was only supposed to be four crystals. North, south, east, and west. That’s what niggled at a corner of her brain.

In her head, she was back in the Egyptian tomb where the crystals had grown. She lifted them from their hiding place. There were six crystals. She had snapped off four; the other two resisted her fingers, and she pushed them back into the niche in the wall. Two extra crystals. *A blue one and a . . .* Susan flapped her hands. *The other one was . . . yellow. Yes, that was it, yellow.*

I wonder how this one got out of the tomb. If this is the Crystal of the Outer Regions, I wonder if the yellow one is the Crystal of the Inner Regions. Susan shuddered. *I’m not sure I want to go there.*

Susan sat up suddenly. The frogs had stopped croaking.

"You're inside an asteroid."

Susan leaped to her feet and turned. The smaller girl stood before her.

"I know that," Susan replied. Then she frowned. "I didn't hear you."

The girl waved her arms toward their camp. "I came to see who you were."

Susan put her hand to her heart. "You startled me."

"Huh." The girl grinned at her. "I sure scared you. I'm quiet in the woods. You're not."

Susan shook herself. "OK, let's start again. Hi, my name is Susan." She smiled at the girl.

"I'm called Squirrel," the girl replied.

Susan nodded. "You mean like the little animal, Squirrel? That collects nuts and lives in trees?"

The girl frowned. "You know what a squirrel is?"

Susan shrugged. "Of course, there are stacks of them in the trees around where I live. We put out peanuts for them. My mum gets mad because they bury them in among her petunias."

The girl stamped her foot and stuck out her chin. "You've never seen a squirrel. You're lying."

Trying to change the subject, Susan huffed out a breath. "You said that we're inside an asteroid. How do you know that?" she asked.

Squirrel put her hands on her hips and glared at Susan. "Don't pretend. How did you get here? There's not supposed to be anyone here but us."

Susan stuck out her chin. "You're not supposed to be here either."

Squirrel bit her lip. She looked as though she might cry.

"Well," Susan said, trying to look friendly. "I've come to help. There's a problem here, and I've come to see if I can help to fix it."

"Throw us out more like." The bigger boy pushed his way out of the bushes to stand beside Squirrel. The bushes rustled again, and the other two children pushed their way through. Susan faced all four children. None looked friendly.

Susan tried another tack. "Where are your parents?"

The first boy answered, "There's just us. We're a secret." He used his thumb to poke his chest. "I'm Badger, that's me. We live in the forest, and we're always going to live here. And you can't make us leave."

Susan spread her arms wide and shrugged. "I'm not trying to make you leave. I don't know who you are or why you're here, but there's a problem that has to be fixed or nobody is going to be living here for long. And anyway, this is one weird place. I still can't get the feel of how it works."

"Ooooh, Karst, the new girl doesn't know much." Badger shoulder-bumped the other boy

Karst's attention jerked back to the group. He'd been staring off into the distance. "Um." He turned all his attention on Susan.

"I will explain," he said, with a nod. "Asteroids, fly around in space." He waved his hand. "Well, actually it's more like they orbit." He straightened his shirt.

Susan noticed that it was worn and frayed along the bottom hem.

The other girl gave a sigh. “Karst, you’re so slow. Just tell it.” She looked at Susan, with a smile. “Brothers.”

“My name is Aurora.” She took up the story. “We’re inside a hollowed-out asteroid. They’re creating a forest in here, with all the trees and animals that used to live all over the Pacific Northwest of what was called North America. There, now you know. Oh yes, we are in space.” Aurora turned to the others. “There you are. That wasn’t so hard to tell, was it?”

Susan pointed up. “So there’s no sky, just more forest?”

Aurora shrugged. “Yep,” she pointed across the pond, “if you just kept walking that way you’d end up up there.” She scratched behind her ear. “It is designed to be eight kilometers in diameter at its widest.”

“But,” Susan wanted to keep them talking, “if we’re in space, why isn’t everything floating? I saw people in the space station, and they had no gravity. Everything floated around.”

“See, smarty. Left that bit out, didn’t you?” Karst sneered at his sister.

Aurora whirled her hands around in a circle. “It’s spinning. That sets up the gravity. It’s called centrifugal force.” Aurora wagged her finger at Susan. “For someone who says she’s here to help us, you don’t know much, do you? Don’t know what help you could be to us.”

"And," Squirrel piped up, "she told me that she has lots of squirrels living around where she lives."

Karst looked quickly at Susan. "Really?"

But at the same time, Badger pushed Susan's shoulder. "Well, that's a lie. We had the only squirrels left on Earth and not many of them."

"What?!" That didn't make sense to Susan. She wasn't lying, but they must be. No squirrels on Earth?

Badger pushed her shoulder again. Susan resisted the temptation to use his momentum to lay him in the mud. *I'm trying to make friends here.*

Badger sneered at her. "Says she's here to help us. Doesn't even know where here is." He motioned to the others with his head. "Come on. We've got things to do. Let's go."

Badger led the way into the bushes. Aurora followed; then Squirrel.

Just as she was disappearing from the clearing, Squirrel reached back and pulled Karst after her into the shrubs.

Susan stood alone.

17

Graveside

Susan sat on the grass again. She pulled at the cool, green blades around her. *I have to admit there's some truth in what Badger said. I don't know anything about this future. I've no clue what's happened on Earth since my time, but it doesn't sound good.* Susan sighed. *The crystal has brought me here, and so I must trust that I have a role to play in keeping New Hope safe, and all the creatures and plants and robots—and even the children—alive and well. And what about the blue crystal and the dead Keeper?*

She pulled up the tuft. The roots smelled earthy and damp. Susan breathed deeply. *There must be something I can do right now.*

Susan climbed to her feet. She pulled her sweatshirt down tight.

She looked around at all the strangeness. She looked up. That pond up there looked so out of place.

Then she realized what she could do. Something she knew about and something that would help in the end. The garden was wrecked by the spacers, but she knew how to work in a vegetable garden. She would go and fix it as best she could. Repairing the damage would give her something helpful to do.

She returned to the smoothed pathway and strode out, heading toward the gardens and the cargo bay entrance. Forward, Sassy had called it.

Susan started out striding along, but the soft shushing of the pine needles and the occasional chatter of birds soon had Susan walking at a much more relaxed pace. That's when she thought of another good reason for her to explore. The more she saw of New Hope, the better she could crystal from place to place. That knowledge could become a safety thing with wolves and bears around.

New Hope was a big place. She wished for her bike. *Maybe Sassy can teach me to drive its train part.* She kept to the path, but her eyes wandered to the side. She was determined to see everything so she could crystal to any spot if she needed to.

Susan was thrilled when she spotted a pair of squirrels. Tails twitching, they chased each other from tree to tree, round and round the trunks, chittering as they ran. *Maybe they lived in cages on Earth.*

Susan stopped still in her tracks. Someone was crying up ahead. Were there more people here? She stepped off the pathway and crept forward.

Peeping through the bushes, she saw the two graves in a clearing. Aurora crouched by the older grave, crying.

Susan wasn't sure what to do. She didn't want to appear to be spying, but she would have to pass the graves to get to the gardens. She crept back to the pathway. Susan scuffed her feet to make noise. She thought of doing a pretend sneeze, but Judy said her sneeze sounded more like a snort. So scuffing along and sort of humming to herself, Susan walked around a curve in the path and arrived at the graves.

Aurora was sitting up and wiping her face by the time Susan arrived graveside.

Susan smiled at her. "I didn't expect to see any of you for a while," she said.

Aurora tried to smile, but it came out crooked. "I had to come here as soon as I could."

Susan came closer and knelt beside her. "Did you know this person?"

Aurora burst into loud sobs. "This is my mother's grave," she wailed.

"Oh." Susan didn't know what to say. Really, there is nothing to say in such circumstances, so Susan scrunched closer and put her arms around Aurora's shoulders and held her tight.

This was exactly the right thing to do. Aurora turned into Susan's chest and sobbed and sobbed. Susan softly stroked her shoulder and rocked a little back and forth. "Shhhhh, shhhhhhh," she whispered.

Aurora sobbed on. Susan stayed quiet, holding her tight. She tried to imagine how she would feel if it was her mother lying in the grave. She shook her head at the horror of it. No more tapping at her statues. No more flea markets. No more forgetting to pass on messages. No more Mum. Wherever Susan was in time, in Egypt, even in space, her mum and dad were at home, safe. Susan hugged Aurora even tighter.

Eventually Aurora's sobs turned to sniffles and, finally, to gulps. She pulled away from Susan and mopped her face on the sleeve of her jacket. She sat quiet, staring at the little cross stuck in one end of the grave. The silence grew too long.

"We could make a stronger cross to put on her grave," Susan suggested.

Aurora started as if she had forgotten Susan was sitting beside her. She sniffed again. "She died of the coughing sickness," she said.

Susan nodded quietly.

"Dad and her brother buried her here. She wanted to come even though she was sick."

"What were they doing here?" Susan hoped to draw Aurora out of her sadness.

Aurora mopped her face again. "They were responsible for making sure the insects and amphibians were settled well and that the whole ecosystem was working as it should."

"So, they were biologists?"

Aurora nodded. "We are one of just a handful of families left on Earth that knows how to occupy and live in a forest like this. At home, we live in one of the few places that still has this ecosystem." Aurora straightened her jacket.

"We look after ten thousand acres of wilderness—the last in the Pacific Northwest."

"That's not much. I live on Vancouver Island, and we have miles of untouched forest."

"You're lying again." Aurora jumped to her feet. "We live on Vancouver Island. It's small, and it's just lucky that a lot of it is owned by one family. And they've restricted access to the area, and we live there and look after it all for them."

Susan stayed seated and made soothing motions with her hands. "Are the owners a couple who play all lovey-dovey with each other, the ones who sold all these animals to the Consortium?"

Aurora fell to her hands and knees in front of Susan. "You know them? The Suttons. Did they send you here?"

"Calm down." Susan made more soothing motions with her hands. "They acted creepy, and from what I saw, they're up to no good."

Aurora frowned at her. "You saw them. Where did you see them? Nobody ever gets into that stronghold they've built for themselves."

"No," Susan assured her, "I saw them on a video screen. It was like a Skype call." Then she sighed.

"There is just so much we don't know about each other." Aurora opened her mouth to speak, but Susan hurried on.

"You have to believe me. There is danger here. I don't know what it is, but something will happen, and you, me, and this whole New Hope place is going to be in trouble if we don't figure out what is wrong and fix it."

Aurora sat back on her heels and glared at Susan. "Humph, you come across as speaking truthfully, but you've told such unbelievable things. Squirrels in your mum's petunias? What are petunias anyway? How did you get here? You're from Vancouver Island? Not likely. It's small, and I know everyone who lives there, all the resort employees and their children, and you're not one of them. Why should I believe you? How can I believe you?"

Susan sat for a moment. Should she tell Aurora about her crystal? That would add another thing that she wouldn't believe.

But Aurora had another question. "Did you kill this Alvion person here?" She waved her hand at the other grave.

Susan's mouth gaped open. "Kill?" She shook her head madly. "The spacers who brought you here killed him, and then the third one came out and buried him."

Aurora slowly nodded. "Badger got a message just before we were put to sleep for the trip. His dad told him that the space pilots had been changed at the last minute. The ones who knew about us were gone. The Suttons made the change."

"They were not good men." Susan stood and dusted off her clothes.

"They wrecked the vegetable garden on their way out. I was on my way to do some repair work when I met you here."

Aurora stood too. "A vegetable garden! They're a big part of our food supply. They must be in working order. There are four, but we need every one."

"Come with me then," Susan said. "We can get to know each other's stories as we work."

"OK."

The two set off along the path together.

Susan had a question straight away. "How did you find the grave so quickly? This place is such a maze, with no sky and no horizons."

Aurora laughed. "It's the ponds. Look at the ponds. The one we are camped by is round and has one island in the middle. It's called Island Pond. The one above and to the right is shaped in a curve. That's Arc Lake. There are four more ponds further aft. Each is a different shape, and they're staggered so that there is not too much weight in any one place; otherwise, the spin would get up a wobble and then we'd really be in trouble. The whole thing would break apart."

"Huh." Susan hadn't given a thought to the pond's shape before. How clever.

Aurora wasn't finished with her explanation though. "There are four pretty straight paths, which lead from fore to aft. The area between each path is known as a quadrant." She pointed like a tour guide. "To the left of where we're walking is the Heinlein quadrant and on the right is the Clark quadrant." Aurora pointed above their heads. "Up there are the Asimov and Le Guin quadrants."

"Stop." Susan laughed. "I feel like my head's on a swivel. I can't take in any more information."

Aurora nodded and smiled. "I can see how that would be."

"Well, you know it all, and you've only been here a day and a night."

Aurora nodded again. "Yes, but we've grown up with our parents poring over the plans for this place. Badger's mum, Agate, is the engineer. My parents and Badger's dad planned and organized the flora and fauna. Us kids all lived, ate, and breathed this place since we could crawl."

They arrived at the garden fence. Aurora stopped in her tracks. She clutched her fingers through the wires. "What a mess."

"Let's hurry then," Susan suggested. "The sooner we can get it put back to rights, the better."

Aurora frowned. "We better check the bee hive first. That's the most important thing."

Susan gasped. "You're right. Do you know where it is?"

Aurora nodded as they swung through the gate.

Susan followed close as Aurora rushed between two garden beds.

There was the hive. Bees buzzed around the entrance.

Aurora bent with her hands on her knees. "They're safe."

The two stood side by side, enjoying the activity of the bees.

Eventually Aurora sighed and looked around. "There's a lot of work needed to fix this mess," she said.

Susan nodded. "But sometimes, having something useful to do is the best way to get through something difficult."

The two set to work.

18

The Garden

Tidying the garden proved to be hard work. The two girls worked quietly side by side, replanting seedlings where they could and repositioning the few remaining tomato plants solidly on their frames. After an hour or so, both were ready for a break.

Susan stood and stretched out her back muscles. Aurora stood beside her. She was a little taller and thinner than Susan.

"I need a drink." Susan groaned.

Aurora nodded. “There should be a tap over there.” She pointed to the orchard.

Once among the trees, they found more destruction. Fallen fruit littered the ground, most of it not even ripe.

Aurora’s shoulders slumped as she surveyed the damage.

“Can we store the fruit somewhere until it ripens?” Susan asked.

“Don’t think so.” Aurora swept her arm around. “Look at this mess. Why would anyone do this to good food?”

The two took turns scooping water into their mouths from the running tap.

“This tastes different from the water at home.” Susan sucked in more from her hand.

Aurora slurped. “It tastes wonderful. Look, it’s clear. It’s running clear.”

“Well, yes, all water is clear.” Susan noticed the look on Aurora’s face. “Isn’t it?”

Aurora screwed up her nose. “Not where I come from,” she said. “We’re among the lucky ones. We live in a forest. There are birds and animals around, but sometimes the rain is dirty or becomes so acidic that it stings your skin. When the sea rose so high, salt got into the water tables and so a lot of the wells became briny. Even in our area, all the water has to be filtered before we can use it, and sometimes we have to boil it too.”

The two sat on a garden seat close to the tap.

Aurora turned to Susan. “Anyway, it can’t be that different where you live. The whole planet is suffering, and nobody is free from the flooding, disease, and pollution. And even if you're from one of the Mars colonies, the environment is still tricky and difficult to live with. Water is even harder there."

Susan sat tongue-tied. What to say? Trust was the thing. Could she trust these children? They weren't supposed to be here. But, they knew more about this place than she did. A slow smile spread across her face. *Of course, I'm here to save New Hope. And these children want it to survive too. Those people in the video call are trying to destroy it. That's the imbalance I am here to help fix. And Alvion too, I want his killers caught.*

Aurora watched the change move across Susan's features. "You just came to a big decision," she murmured, and smiled too.

Susan took a deep breath. It was time to explain. And so she did. She hauled the crystals out of her pocket, half hoping that the blue one would fly into Aurora's hand. That didn't happen, but Aurora saw them and poked the crystals with her finger, causing lights to dance between the two. Aurora pulled a string out of her blouse and showed Susan the crystal attached to the end of it. A red one, exactly the same as the one Judy wore. Susan gulped back a wave of homesickness, thinking of Judy outside, waiting to light the candles on her birthday cake. *I'll probably be twelve instead of eleven by the time I get home from here,* Susan thought.

Susan explained why she had the crystals and how she time-slipped to fix things. Aurora nodded her head slowly as Susan spoke.

Finally, with her story told, Susan sat still, staring at her hands folded in her lap.

"I believe you," Aurora said and patted Susan gently on the shoulder.

Susan looked up startled. "You do?"

"I do." Aurora grinned. "Uncle Heath, Badger and Squirrel's dad, collects any old books he can find. Whenever he has to leave and travel to meetings or conventions, he always brings back a few. And Karst is deep into the internet. We get good service where we are—were—because the resort has a dedicated satellite overhead. Karst built himself a backdoor into the system and finds all sorts a wonderful stories there.

Most of the really good ones come from the times before the Great Exit." Aurora poked Susan in the ribs. "I've probably read stories about you."

Susan shrugged. "Nobody will write stories about me. What I do is secret."

Aurora burst out laughing. "Susan, you might think so, but I've read stories about Crystal Keepers, so there."

"But not me," Susan insisted.

Aurora laughed again. "I'm not saying," she said.

19

Where's Sassy?

Susan and Aurora found a large basket and filled it with the fallen fruit. They picked up a few edible peaches lying on the ground, and once again, sitting by the tap, the two shared the fruit, eating around the bruised parts.

Aurora ran her tongue all over the palm of her hand. She sucked each finger to get the last possible lick of juice. "We have peaches at home, if we're really lucky, and the guests don't eat them all," she told Susan between licks. "But these have a different flavor. They taste cleaner somehow."

Susan ran her hands under the tap. "Well, the dirt is crushed up asteroid. No human has ever touched it until these trees were planted. And I know the water came from an asteroid too." She shrugged. "That feels so weird to me."

Aurora laughed again. "Oh, Susan, there are so many gaps in what you know."

"Well, I know things that you don't too." Susan defended herself, drying her hands on her jeans.

Aurora opened her mouth to speak again, but then seemed to think better of it. She paused. She looked deep into Susan's eyes. Then she slowly nodded her head. "You know, you are so right. We know stuff about here, but you know a lot of stuff about before when Earth was more livable."

Susan spread her hands wide. "So just think how smart we'll be when we all work together to keep this wonderful place safe."

Aurora leaped off the seat and gave Susan a huge hug. "You're right," she said. "The Crystal Keeper only ever goes to places where there is an imbalance that must be fixed. There must be a problem here." She looked around. "Except for what the spacers did to the garden, everything seems to be just the way it was planned. There doesn't look to be any danger." But then her shoulders slumped again. "Oh, I was forgetting about the other grave. The other Crystal Keeper." She looked all around. "We must find the danger. We must fix it. We need to be safe."

The two began dragging the basket full of ruined fruit toward the garden gate. It was heavy.

"I wish this thing had wheels." Aurora grunted.

Susan stood up and stretched her back. "We need Sassy."

"Sassy? Who's Sassy? Is there someone else here we don't know about?" Aurora looked over her shoulder as if she expected to see someone hiding behind the runner beans.

It was Susan's turn to laugh. "It's OK." She made calming motions with her hands. "I have to think for a moment."

Aurora tapped her foot while her eyes roved all around.

"Sassy is the name I gave to a . . ." Susan flapped her fingers, "a semi-stealth autonomous storage device. I call it Sassy for short."

"A robot?"

"More like a box with lights." Susan laughed. "But it talks to me and shows me around in the tunnels. Partition 'tasked' it with being my guide." Susan used air quotes around tasked.

"And who," Aurora swept a bow in Susan's direction, "may Partition be?"

"I called it Partition. Alvion True partitioned off a section of the AI for his use and also upgraded Sassy from just a storage device."

"You talked to Alvion True?"

Susan shook her head. "No, the spacers shot him before I arrived. I wouldn't have been drawn here if he wasn't dead."

"But you know stuff."

"He recorded a message for whoever followed him. Sassy and Partition played it for me." Susan pulled out the crystals again.

"That's his blue one stuck to mine. I was hoping it would find a new Keeper."

Aurora poked it gently. "I would be so proud to be the Keeper of the Crystal of the Outer Regions."

Susan closed her hand over both of them. "The crystals choose their own Guardians. It did react to you a little, so maybe something will happen"

Aurora shook herself and sighed. "Let's get this fruit out where the birds and animals can get at it. Better not to waste it."

But Susan stood still. She'd just remembered. "There's more. Those men did more. I forgot to tell you. The third one attached himself to a computer panel on the wall of the cargo bay, and he uploaded stuff. He said he was infiltrating the AI. It was him the owners most wanted to talk to when they appeared on the screen."

Aurora looked alarmed. "The owners talked. What did they say? It's important. They made a fortune from the contract to create the ecosystem here, but they never wanted this place built. This place will cut into the huge profits from their resort."

Susan tried to think back, but the worry on Aurora's face left her feeling so agitated she couldn't think straight. "We should ask Sassy. It said it didn't record what I saw, but it can probably report exactly what I heard. It showed me what was happening on a big screen in the tunnel." Susan looked around. "Where is Sassy? It's my guide. I haven't seen it since

I came down the slope to talk to you." She felt a bit abandoned. "Maybe now that I'm with you, it doesn't want to help me anymore."

Aurora waved her hand. "Well Sassy or not, Karst is the one we need to set onto the computer. He can make them sing. We should get him and take him to the panel you saw the guy hooked into."

Susan nodded. "Um, I think I can find the place." She waved behind them. "It was the other side of the garden. There's a path leading up to the cargo bay."

Aurora nodded. "I know where that is. Let's get the others."

The two set off through the gate and ran along the path, the basket of fruit forgotten.

"The sooner we can get Karst to figure out what the guy did to AI, the sooner we can get it back on track." Aurora panted.

Past the graves they loped and onward toward Island Pond and the cages.

20

Where is Everybody?

They arrived at the camp puffing. The carefully arranged cages were pulled apart. The canvas roof was torn down the middle. No children were in sight.

Aurora huffed, hands on hips. “Come out. This isn’t funny.”

No answer. The birds and frogs stopped their noise as if listening for the children too.

The two girls stood back to back, their eyes searching the surrounding trees.

"Could those men have returned?" Susan whispered.

Aurora shrugged. "Don't think so. Why would they?"

They stood together, rigid in place.

"Maybe we should check the animals. When were the bears going to wake?"

Aurora gasped. "No, no," she murmured. "Karst! Badger! Squirrel!" she yelled.

"Sshhhhhh, AI will hear you."

The two girls ducked down. Their heads pivoted all around.

"Did you hear that?" Aurora whispered.

Susan nodded. "It sounded a bit like Sassy. But I can't see it."

"What does it look like?"

"A box. Sort of grayish, with little lights all around about two inches down from the top."

"I'm over here by the pond," a small voice squeaked.

"Sassy, is that you?" Susan tried to call quietly.

"Be quiet, keep low, but come get me, quickly."

The girls crouched and crept toward the pond.

"Do you think your Sassy did something to the others?" Aurora asked.

"I doubt it. Sassy knew you were here. I told it."

Susan hurried ahead to the pond. "It'll probably know what happened, though, and where the others are."

They stood on the edge of the water and looked out across the pond. No grayish box anywhere.

"Come and get me, quickly," Sassy called.

Aurora pointed off to the right. "Look, the reeds are disturbed over there."

The girls hurried over to the spot, and there, on its side, lay Sassy. Water lapped at one corner of the box, and its little wheels were spinning uselessly as it tried to right itself.

"Sassy, what happened?" Susan stepped into the water and pushed the reeds aside.

"Get me out of here. I'm getting wet. Two of my storage compartments are already full of water."

"Where are the others?" Aurora demanded.

"Hurry, hurry, my circuits are close to the water level."

Susan put her hands under Sassy's lowest corner. She heaved. Sassy wobbled, but didn't budge.

"Help me." Susan waved her head at Aurora.

"I want to know where the others are." Aurora stuck out her chin.

Susan sighed in exasperation. "Well, if Sassy's circuits fry, it will take us a lot longer to find out, won't it? Help me."

Aurora sloshed into the water on the other side, and between the two of them, they managed to get Sassy upright. That wasn't the end of the problem, though. It was still stuck in the reeds. Sassy's wheels couldn't get any purchase in the mud.

Susan bent down to check out the problem. Sassy's wheels were too small. "You were certainly built for traveling on the paths and in the tunnels, Sassy." She patted his lid. "You're still stuck, but at least you're upright and out of the water."

Aurora leaned over and rapped her knuckles on Sassy's side. "So tell us, now you're upright. Where. Are. The others?"

Sassy's light display flashed red, and then the lights ran around its circumference. "I tried to stop them. I truly did."

"WHAT HAPPENED?" The two girls shouted together.

21

What Happened?

Sassy sighed. "AI happened."

"That tells us everything, doesn't it?" Susan cocked her head at the little box.

"What happened?"

"Partition found out what AI was going to do just before it gave the commands, so Partition told me to hurry down and warn the children. But I can only travel on the paths, and it was a long way around to the inter-sector pathway. I hurried; I truly did.

I got to the path just over there." Sassy pointed to the pathway closest to the boxes.

"I called out to the children. 'Hide. Hide,' I called. The big boy came out and looked at me. He looked around.

I waved my arm and jiggled in place. I even used my big voice, but he ignored me and went back inside their box circle.

"Then the others came. Our segment fifty-sixes are engineered to travel in rough terrain. They have big wheels. They are used for heavy maintenance throughout the biosphere. AI sent two. I tried to stop them. I charged right into the first in line." Sassy used its arm to feel along one side of itself. "I think I have a dent."

The girls leaned forward. They didn't want to miss a word of Sassy's story.

"I yelled and yelled and the children burst out of their circle to see what was going on. The fifty-sixes grabbed them. They didn't even have time to run."

"But how did the boxes get thrown around and the roofing split?" Aurora wanted to know.

"They were looking for the fourth child. They knew there should be four, but they only caught three."

Susan nudged at Aurora. "I bet my cloaking covered us both."

Sassy jigged in place. "Yes, that's it. But the fifty-sixes didn't know about the cloaking, so they were really confused about not finding number four." Sassy's lights flashed orange and red in sequence. "That's when Leviathan One's fifty-six picked me up and shook me. I'm sorry, but I spilled your lunch,

Susan. But I didn't tell them what I know, and that's when it threw me aside.

I landed in the reeds." Sassy shuddered all over. "I think it was aiming for the water." Susan stroked its top.

"They wheeled off with the three children."

"Where are the children now?" Susan looked around. *Thirty-five kilometers long, eight kilometers in diameter. All the tunnels, control rooms, accommodation.* Susan sighed. *They could be anywhere.*

Sassy's golden lights ran around his edges. "Partition is endeavoring to find out, Susan."

Aurora piped up. "We need to get Sassy back on the pathways so that we can get away from here."

Susan nodded, but she looked at the clumpy expanse of ground between where they stood and the pathway. "How?"

Aurora walked over to the line of cages. "Some are made to come apart, but they all hold the larger animals that haven't been released yet."

What could they use? Susan glimpsed the torn roofing. It flapped gently in the slight breeze. "What about that?" she asked pointing.

"Yes. Perfect." Aurora shoulder-bumped her, and they hurried over to the flapping canvas.

Susan ran her hand over the material. It felt like a stiff tarp.

"It folded up in my nest for the trip," Aurora told her. "Once we arrived and straightened it out, Badger had a spray in his nest, which made it stiffen like this."

Susan nodded as the two lifted the length down and carried it over to lay as a path. It drifted in the air; it was so light. "You really planned this move very well, didn't you?"

Aurora nodded as they placed it carefully over the ground. From Sassy, it didn't reach all the way to the path. The girls went back for the other piece.

"It's our parents who planned it. You have no idea how horrible it is on Earth now. Most people have no work and no homes. They live in huge, scary camps. Just a few people own everything. If you're lucky, like our parents, you have a skill and can work for them, but they pay you in credit, and that only lets you get things from their stores, so you can never get away or out of debt to them. You're indentured; you owe them everything."

Susan stopped short and stood with her mouth open. She gulped. "But what about the government? What are they doing?"

Aurora shrugged. "They do what they can, but there are millions and millions of people homeless. Everyone had to move inland as the seas rose and the rivers flooded. The ports and coastal cities all went under water."

"But, surely the government is helping the people and getting things working."

Aurora shrugged again. "They try. Some are more successful than others. But they have no money for extra services. It's hard to find land that will grow enough food."

"But people are rich. You said so." Susan spread her arms wide.

"Yep, I did. But somehow those people have ways of not paying taxes or contributing in any way." Aurora sighed.

Susan shuddered. "Like those Suttons."

Aurora nodded. "Exactly. I hope that one day it will all sort itself out and Earth will be a good place again. But not for a long time yet."

"Ahem, I think we need to hurry." Sassy snapped its lid up and down to get their attention.

The two girls jumped at the interruption.

"Sorry, Sassy," Susan said and hurried to lift down the next piece of roofing. *I will have to think about what Aurora told me later.*

Then she gasped.

Nanaimo probably isn't even there anymore.

The girls carried the second piece over to finish the path. Aurora continued with her story. "Our parents organized the biosphere here. They had skills with the forest and the animals. They nurture the flora and fauna at the Sutton Range Resort on Earth. But all the money that the Consortium paid for their work, here, went to the Suttons. We lived better than others, but not that much better. Our parents wanted us to be free."

Together the girls lifted Sassy onto their makeshift path. Slowly, it moved toward the pathway. In some places, the two had to give it a little push over a bumpy spot, but it made progress.

Suddenly Sassy stopped short. It was totally silent for a moment, but Susan could tell by the color and movement of its lights that Sassy was agitated.

"Quickly, quickly, hide. Partition relayed to me that AI is sending a fifty-six to keep watch. It is almost here."

"Will you be alright?" Susan lightly touched Sassy's top.

"Yes, yes, go. Hide well." Sassy waved its arm at them.

Susan and Aurora ran into the forest.

22

Jacket Swap

Susan pulled Aurora down into the bushes at the edge of the clearing. They both watched as a robot rolled into view. To Susan, it looked about the size of a smart car. Two grasper arms protruded from its front. Its wheels were large and had soft tires.

Aurora pointed and whispered in Susan's ear. "That's so it can go off the paths without harming the vegetation."

Susan nodded, her eyes glued to the scene by the pond.

Sassy still struggled slowly over the roofing material. The fifty-six rolled over and lifted it with its two forward arms.

Two extra arms unfolded from its box-like body, and these went under Sassy, supporting it, as the fifty-six wheeled over to the path and lowered it onto the smooth surface.

Susan watched Sassy's lights. They moved lazily back and forth across the surface facing the fifty-six. They showed a calm pale green. Gradually the lights of the two robots synced so that the color and the rhythm of their movements matched each other.

"It's like they've reached some sort of agreement," Susan whispered to Aurora.

The fifty-six gave Sassy a gentle push along the path and turned back toward the clearing. It swiveled its top-most section, as though scanning the surroundings.

Carefully, quietly, Susan and Aurora crawled backwards through the undergrowth until they were far enough away to stand and run.

"Where are we going?" Aurora panted.

"Can we reach the grave area without using the path?" Susan panted back.

Aurora grabbed Susan's sleeve and turned their direction just a little. The two ran together.

They would reach the graves before Sassy, or so Susan hoped.

The two crouched low in the shrubs surrounding the clearing. Aurora clutched at her chest as their breathing slowed to normal.

"Are you OK?" Susan patted her shoulder.

Aurora nodded. "I'll be alright. It's just that the air on Earth, even where we lived, is polluted, so we try not to exert ourselves too much in the unfiltered areas. We don't get much running practice." She puffed. "We tried to train for here, but it had to be secret. We'll build up stamina the longer we're here."

Susan sat back against the trunk of a tree. She tried to imagine living on the Earth of this time. She had seen the newscasts of pollution enveloping, New Delhi and Beijing, but now she had to think about what it would be like to live in that her whole life. To be born in it and live in it. Susan shook her head sadly.

She remembered a time Judy and she rode their bikes to the top of the nearest peak. They were puffing when they reached the top, but when they looked out to the east, they could see all the land below them, across Georgia Strait to the Mainland and all the snow-capped peaks, stretching into the distance. She quirked her mouth, thinking of how they had taken it for granted. They'd given no thought to the possibility that in a few hundred years, they wouldn't be able to ride their bikes to the peak or see across the water.

Aurora was watching her.

Susan started back to the here and now.

"I can hear wheels on the pathway," Aurora whispered.

Susan nodded, and the two watched avidly, hoping it would be Sassy that rounded the corner.

And it was.

The girls left the trees and walked out into the clearing around the graves. Sassy whirred to a stop.

"Ah, I hoped I would see you," it said.

"Does the fifty-six know where the children are?" Sassy's lights blinked briefly. "No, AI sent my fifty-six and ordered it to watch for the other child."

Susan squatted beside Sassy, and as she did, the crystals in her pocket poked into her thigh. *Huh.*

"Sassy, does AI know what Aurora looks like?"

Sassy was quiet for a moment, its lights whirling.

"Partition thinks not. AI is still searching."

Susan stood. "OK, I've got a plan—I think." She turned to Aurora. "Swap jackets with me."

"Why?"

Susan already had her sweatshirt off. She handed it to Aurora.

"So that AI will think I'm you."

"Why?" Aurora began shrugging out of her jacket.

Susan grinned at her. "I'm about to do Crystal Guardian stuff."

Aurora jumped to her feet. "Really? You have a plan?"

Susan nodded. "Really. Sassy, can you take Aurora to the room I slept in last night?"

Sassy bobbed formally. "Yes, Crystal Keeper, I can conduct Aurora to that location."

"Good, keep her cloaked and uncloak me. I'll see you there." Susan slipped Aurora's jacket on and headed to the camp.

"Good luck," she heard as she rounded the bend.

23

Rescue

Susan rushed over to the overturned boxes, yelling and flapping her hands. "Oh, Oh, where is everyone?" she yelled as loud as she could.

As expected, the fifty-six rolled out of the trees and placed one gripper on her shoulder. A heavy gripper.

"Come," it said.

"Where," Susan squeaked in her most scared little girl voice. "Where are my cousins and my brother?"

She flapped her hands and danced from foot to foot. "They need me," she added.

The fifty-six said no more. It picked her up and tucked her under one of its arms. It rolled along the path in the opposite direction to the gravesite.

Susan kept a firm grip on the crystals. *If it gets too dangerous, I can always leap to the vegetable garden.* She settled in for an uncomfortable ride. Hanging upside down in the fifty-six's grip was nobody's idea of first class robot travel.

She kept as close a look-out as she could, though. The more she could learn of New Hope, the better she would be able to get around. As the fifty-six was heading aft, Susan spied the next set of ponds. The land was laid out to be clearings and then forests and then another clearing. The path ran almost straight.

Eventually they reached an intersection, and the fifty-six turned to the right and headed off in a new direction. They reached a small landing, and from there, a fold opened and they traveled into the tunnels. The fifty-six picked up speed and zoomed along. Susan shut her eyes tight. It was too fast for her to catch any detail. The robot used no lights anyway. Its arm pressed into her stomach, and she had to wriggle her legs every now and again just be sure they were still there.

I wonder if it would stop and put me down if I threw up on its wheels, Susan thought.

She was about to find out when the fifty-six screeched to a halt. A segment of the wall to their left unfolded to reveal a small dimly-lit room. Three children sat in a group, huddled on the floor. Badger sprang to his feet and rushed forward with his fists up.

"The other one," the fifty-six announced and dropped Susan at Badger's feet. Badger stumbled over her in his rush for the door. The fifty-six wheeled out backwards, and the door folded shut.

Badger kicked out at her. "Get out of my way."

It was too late; the exit disappeared.

Susan groaned and rolled onto her back. Pins and needles attacked her legs and arms.

Karst crawled over to where Susan sat trying to massage the feeling back into her limbs. "Aurora's jacket." He fingered the weave on the collar. "But not Aurora." He pinched her ear. "You again. Where's Aurora?"

Susan pulled away from his fingers. "Ow." She slapped his hand. "Be quiet. They could be listening." She beckoned the others together. "Help me get rid of these pins and needles, please."

Squirrel moved forward and began rubbing at her calves.

"Aurora's safe. I've come to rescue you," Susan whispered when they were all gathered round.

"Spy on us, more like," Badger muttered, but Susan noticed he kept his voice low.

Susan sighed. "You are one suspicious person. Do you know that?" She frowned at Badger.

"It's his training," Squirrel piped up. "They were going to make him a part of the security police patrol for the resort. They were training him to be suspicious."

Badger cleared his throat. "Well, I don't know how you think you're going to rescue us, little bitty girl, no bigger than Aurora. Got caught by a robot."

"I sure did," Susan responded. "We couldn't figure out where they were holding you, so this was the only way to get you out."

Badger flapped his hand dismissively. "Sure, sure. I've gone over every centimeter of this room. They control the exit with its silly folds; there's no controls in here. I can't even figure out where the air is coming in. So, little girl, I don't know what you're going to do."

Susan rolled her eyes and shook her head. "Maybe I'll leave you behind to figure your own way out."

It's hard to put a lot of scorn in your voice when you're whispering, but Badger rocked back on his heels and pinched his lips closed.

Susan got down to business. "When was the last time you had food?"

Karst answered. "It was two hours and forty-three minutes ago."

Squirrel jerked her head toward him. "We call him computer-head," she said.

Susan nodded. "Right, we'll wait until they bring food again, and then we'll go. That way it could be a long time before they realize we're on the loose."

"Humph, pretty confident, aren't you?" Badger walked over to the wall and slouched down in the corner. Squirrel followed.

Susan moved too, although she stood and stretched out her back and arms. It felt good to get the kinks out after her robot ride. Badger watched her for a while and then rose and joined her. Susan noticed that he was limber for a boy who was so tall and bulky on his frame.

"Have you noticed any spy cameras in the room?" Susan whispered to Badger as they both bent forward to lay their hands on the floor.

"No, but I can't detect the door once it folds shut either," Badger replied.

"Has the AI asked you questions?"

Badger shook his head. "Nothing. Grabbed us. Hauled us here. Dumped us. Food was already here."

The dim lights dimmed further and then further. Then they went out.

"I guess it figures it's sleep time." Susan gave a final stretch.

Badger pulled a small flashlight from his pocket. Then wound a small handle to brighten the light.

"Sometimes old ideas work best," he told Susan.

The four gathered in one corner of the room. Squirrel climbed into Badger's lap and put her head on his shoulder. "I want to go home," she whispered. "I miss Mum and Dad."

"I know." Badger gently rubbed her back.

Susan let the quiet settle over the group. *Maybe it would be better if I just waited until they fell asleep and then moved us.* She shook her head. *They've suffered a lot of shocks and surprises in the last few hours. They don't need another one.*

"Right," she whispered. "Time to go."

"Uh, huh," Badger murmured. "Go where? Back to Sutton Range Resort? No thanks."

"I was thinking of joining Aurora and solving your problems so that New Hope and you can all survive, actually."

Susan pulled the crystals from her pocket. Hers sparkled in the dark. "Make sure we are all touching," she ordered. Karst moved in closer to Squirrel. Susan put her arm around his back. Then hand-holding the crystals, she lay her hand on Badger's knee. She noticed the look of disbelief on his face. *Oh, that's about to change.* She chuckled to herself.

The room where she slept. The bed, with the lovely soft duvet with the humming bird picture. The ablution area. Oh yes, that will be needed. She drew the picture in her mind, forming a solid image of the room. The smell. The sound. The feel.

"Crystal, take us there," she instructed. The room smeared. The walls whirled a little. Karst made a small whimpering sound.

They landed on the bed in the room. Badger was too close to the edge and rolled off onto the floor, with Squirrel held tight in his arms. Karst leaped to his feet and ran to give Aurora a huge hug.

"Whoohoo," he crowed. "Can we do that again?"

Susan watched the excited group hug as the cousins all began talking at once. Alone, she crept into the ablution area. She sat on the toilet seat. She needed to take a couple of deep breaths. A slow smile crept across her face. She did it. She rescued the children. But now what?

Susan noticed that her grip on the crystals was so tight her fingers were cramping. She pried her hand open. There lay her crystal sparkling up at her. The blue one still clung to its side. She realized, with a start, that she hadn't thought about the blue.

What if it hadn't moved with them? Would it have mattered? Susan wasn't sure. *So much I still don't know*.

She shook her head. And then she just sat, enjoying the quiet.

24

Karst Knows Humphrey

The door burst open.

"There she is," Aurora declared, pointing. "Come out. We want you in our hug."

Susan jumped up. All four children were beaming at her. *Thank goodness I was just using the toilet as a seat. I guess this is what it's like living in a large family group.*

She moved out into the main room. The aroma of freshly-cooked food wafted around. Susan sniffed the air. Tomato sauce, melted cheese, mushrooms.

Sassy stood with its top lid open. Susan peeped in. Pizza. Excellent.

Everyone clustered around to grab a slice.

Susan realized that she hadn't made the bed when she jumped out this morning, so she took the time to spread out the duvet so that everyone could sit comfortably while they ate.

With her own slice in her hand, Susan moved over. The four children stood, staring at the bed. Karst made a sudden deep sucking noise and clutched at Aurora's waist. Aurora sank to the floor and gathered Karst to her, pizza forgotten.

"What's happened?" Susan asked Badger.

He waved his pizza slice at the bed cover. "It's their mum's duvet. This must have been her room when she worked up here." Badger moved to sit in the corner on the floor. Squirrel, ever curious, moved over to the mirror against one wall. She fiddled with the articles resting on a shelf. "Oh," she picked up a brush, "look, it's Auntie Spruce's." She carried it across the room and handed it to Aurora, who ran her fingers gently through the bristles.

Karst looked up at her. "Do you think this is where she died?" he asked.

Aurora shook her head. "No, Karst, you've heard the story many times from Dad and from Uncle Heath. Mum died by Central Pond with the beaver dam on it."

Karst sighed. "I miss her."

"We all miss her, Karst." Badger said softly. "But we're here now, and as soon as we sort out a few things, we will all go and take some flowers to her grave. Will that help?"

Karst nodded just once. He sat up and wiped his face on his sleeve. "Is there any pizza left?" He looked around. Sassy had its lid firmly closed.

Susan walked over and tapped gently on its lid. "I was just keeping it warm," it said, and the lid creaked open.

"Great pizza, by the way." Susan took another slice. "Is there anything to drink?"

"There are juice containers in my rear lower compartment." Sassy turned to show Susan where. "I restocked while you were busy," it added.

"And you got your little flap fixed, too, I see." Susan touched the spot where the compartment door had been unhinged.

"I needed some servicing after my dunking. I visited the maintenance area."

"Well, you look fine now."

"I thought you said there was some urgency in fixing this problem." Badger reached for more pizza. "So why are you chit-chatting with a box?"

"This is Sassy." Susan introduced it. "It has been a great help to me, and you'd all be getting hungry and thirsty about now if it wasn't for Sassy."

Squirrel walked over and patted Sassy's side. "Are you a he or a she?" she asked.

Sassy pulled back a little. "I'm a storage device. I have no he or she. I am me," it declared.

Susan put an arm around her shoulder. "I'll explain to you later about what the robots around here are and where they came from."

She turned to Karst. "I hear you are skilled with computers."

Karst looked up and nodded.

"I think that's exactly what we need right now." Susan sat on the floor, and the others scrunched down around her. She explained about what she had seen.

About the men with the cages. That they'd killed Alvion True. But mostly she told about what Humphrey had said about tampering with the AI.

They all listened carefully, nodding, and scowling along with her story. As soon as Susan mentioned Humphrey and his actions, Karst started fiddling with the collar of his shirt.

There was silence for a moment when she finished telling about the Sutton's communication.

It was Karst who broke the silence. "I know Humphrey. He was my trainer at the resort."

Aurora pulled back from the group. "That Humphrey?"

"Huh?" Badger chipped in. "Yes, Sirrah. No, Sirrah. Anything you want, Sirrah. That Humphrey?"

Aurora nodded. "Well, we all know how slimy he is, but we also know how good he is with computers and AI."

She turned to Karst. "Do you think you can figure out what he did? Do you think you can reverse it?"

Karst nodded, but his face didn't show full confidence. "I'll have to look and see if I can track his actions." He pulled open his collar. Susan saw he had a connector implanted there. She tried not to shudder. Her neck itched in that spot.

Badger leaned over and patted Karst's shoulder. "Good thing you had that fitted before we took off, big guy," he said.

Susan stood. "What do you need to get started?"

"An interface like Humphrey used, I guess."

Susan turned to Sassy. "Is it safe for us to be in the cargo bay?"

Sassy's lights flashed red. "There is too much oversight from bits of me and the others in the cargo bay, Susan. Many are connected directly to AI.

"What about the place you took me first? Control Room B or was it C?"

"Ah, perfect. I'll inform Partition that we are on our way."

"Um, are you and Partition able to cloak all of us?"

Sassy waved its arm. "We handled that. You are all covered for now."

Susan gestured with her hand. "Well then, lead the way."

Sassy rushed at the wall. "Not through the service tunnels," Susan reminded it.

"But, that's the shortest way."

Susan waved at the children standing around. "Shortest, but not quickest." She walked to the other wall which unfolded. "This way please," she said and walked out into the tunnel beyond.

25

Mule Deer?

Ah, Partition greeted them as they stepped into Control Room B, Susan of the Crystal accompanied by four mule deer—and Sassy.

Susan looked around quickly. "There's mule deer?"

The others quickly moved out of the door opening and backed up to the walls.

You didn't explain, Sassy?

Sassy rocked back and forth. "Um, I didn't get a chance."

Susan stepped in. “Partition, explain please. We would all like to know.”

Partition’s voice gentled. You’ve named me ‘Partition’?

Susan nodded. “It felt appropriate that you should have a name too.”

Partition sighed. Thank you, it murmured.

Badger stepped forward next. “Explain the four mule deer that aren’t here.”

Ah, one of my mule deer. Welcome to New Hope, young Sirrah. I value your addition to our ecosystem.

Squirrel stamped her foot. “Explain! I need to know!”

Smallest mule deer. I will do so. I was not able to cloak you as I have Susan. I can only do that for one or two people. AI is extremely disturbed that four extra cages arrived. I calculated your combined weight, oxygen consumption and use of water, and extrapolated from that which animals would best cover that drain on resources. Two year old mule deer with two fawns best matched my calculations. So, you are inserted into AI’s knowledge stream as such. You may carry on as normal.

Badger tugged his jacket down. “Humph, just so long as I don’t sprout antlers, I guess that will work.”

Aurora pushed Karst forward.

“Partition, I am known as Aurora. We have brought Karst here with us. He will try to trace the interference that Humphrey uploaded into AI.”

Step forward, Mule Deer Karst. Are you able to interface directly with my systems?

Karst looked around, nodding slowly. "You are amazing," he whispered.

Why, thank you, little one. Plug in. Let's see how we can work together.

AI seems confused in some segments. The interference of Humphrey was not scheduled and AI has no recollection of it happening.

Karst reached for his shirt collar. Susan quickly looked away. She heard the zzzt of the cord unfurling from him neck. Squirrel patted her hand. "You get used to it," she whispered.

Susan looked around at the others. Karst was already plugged into the wall socket that Sassy had used before. His face looked blank. But his eyes were alive. His body was still, but there was a feeling of excitement about him. Aurora had her hand on his shoulder. She beckoned Sassy over. "He can't stand like this for too long. He needs to be sitting and supported."

Sassy sighed. "I will summon a seating arrangement. I have one of me quite close." It sighed again. "In the meantime, I will help." Sassy slipped up behind Karst.

Aurora placed her hand on Sassy's lid. "May I?" she asked. She held up her mother's duvet. The one with the humming bird on it.

Sassy sighed. "Very well." It agreed.

Quickly, Aurora spread the duvet over Sassy. It nudged gently against Karst. Aurora lifted him into a sitting position on Sassy's lid. Sassy hunkered down. Karst took no notice of any of this. His eyes were closed now, but his whole body looked electric.

Badger paced the room. "I have stuff to do. Our camp's a mess. I need to be watching the animals.

I have to be sure they're all hidden before the predators are released."

He counted the tasks off on his fingers. "Besides there's nothing for me to do here." He waved his arm around the room. "I need some air. I hate these tunnels."

Squirrel ran over. "I'll help you," she said.

They both turned to Susan. Badger raised his eyebrows and jerked his head toward the door.

26

What's a Chiptat?

"It's this way."

Susan waved her arm to the left and started off along the tunnel.

Badger caught her arm. "Wait, I want to crystal to the camp."

Squirrel jumped up and down. "Oooh, that would be brill. I like the dizzy-wizzy feeling."

Susan frowned and, hands on hips, confronted the two. "I'm not a circus act you know."

"Ah, come on." Badger's face took on a pleading look. "How often will we get to crystal around?"

He crooked his finger to his thumb, making a small space between. “Just one little crystal hop for us? We might never get to do it again.”

Susan huffed, amused. “Probably by the time we get stuff sorted out in here, we will have all done more ‘crystalling’ than we want.”

“Please, please.” Squirrel wrapped her arms around Susan’s waist.

Susan chuckled. “Gather round.” She gestured with her arms to pull Badger in too.

They huddled close to her. And waited.

“What’s happening?” Badger pulled his head back to look at her. “Why haven’t we moved?”

“Hold on,” Susan responded. “It’s not magic, you know. I have to get everything just right to ensure we get where we want to go.”

“Humph.”

Squirrel giggled.

Susan formed a firm picture in her mind of the pond. The cages. The torn roof. The messed up reeds where they rescued Sassy. And then they went.

“Brill!” Squirrel squealed and jumped up and down on the spot.

“Pretty good.” Badger tried to act cool, but Susan saw the excitement in his eyes.

The thrill soon died when they looked around the wrecked campsite though. More of the cages were open now, but fortunately the bears and cougars were still in deep sleep.

Badger spread his arms wide and smiled at Susan. “Welcome to Camp Bask,” he said. He looked around. “Such as it is,” he grumbled.

To lighten the mood, Susan gave a quick curtsey. "Thank you, sir," she said. "Bask?" she added.

Squirrel skipped up. "Badger, Aurora, Squirrel, and Karst," she said.

Badger shrugged. "Our parents called it Haven, but we wanted our own name for it."

Badger wandered over to the roofing material spread on the grass for Sassy's track. He pulled up one piece and looked down at the other length.

"Will you be able to mend it?" Susan asked, coming up behind him.

Badger shrugged. "I think so." He turned to Squirrel, who was running along the top of the cages. "Squirrel, find the otter cage and bring back the supplies from it," he ordered.

Squirrel danced a couple of steps and then continued her run along the cages. Susan could hear her singing as she went. "Otter, otter cage, where are you? Otter, otter cage, where are you?"

Squirrel almost reached the end of the line before she let out a squeal. "Found it," she called.

Meanwhile, Badger rolled the lengths into two bundles. He carried them to a fresh area of grass and laid them out, side by side. He matched up the torn edges, with just a little overlap.

Squirrel arrived carrying a bag slung over her shoulder. She dropped it beside Badger.

"Thanks, squirt," he acknowledged, without getting up from where he crouched. "Start pulling our stuff out of the open cages. And bring the smaller ones down to our four. Do you remember how they stack?"

"Of course I do. We only did it about a million zillion times to practice," she retorted. She took a couple of steps back along the line. She turned back.

"Do you want to come and help me, Susan?" She beckoned.

"Sure, why not?" Susan joined her, and they set off along the line of cages.

They decided to start at the end and work back toward the camp area.

Squirrel was eager to explain what they were doing. "Our mums and dads planned all this. Each cage was built a little bit bigger than necessary."

Chipmunk showed on the label of one cage. "Chipmunks like to cuddle together. There were probably five in this box. This size would have fitted eight," Squirrel said as she moved to the back of the box. Susan barely made out three small marks on the surface. Squirrel carefully placed her fingers on the marks, and a compartment opened under her fingers.

Squirrel reached in and pulled out a package wrapped in foil. She handed it to Susan. They moved on to the next box. And on and on, until Susan's arms ached from the load she carried.

Each cage had a different opening method, and the secret supplies were hidden in different ways from box to box. But Squirrel never hesitated. At each cage, she quickly removed what was hidden within. Eventually Susan had to protest.

"Squirrel, I can't carry any more. We need to take this lot back to camp."

"Oh, sorry. This is such fun. I remembered it all." Squirrel pulled some of the load from Susan's arms, and together they sat for a moment to rest.

"I miss Mum and Dad." Squirrel rubbed her head on Susan's shoulder. "I felt safe with them," she said.

"You are young to be away from your family." Susan patted her shoulder. "Why did you have to leave so soon? Couldn't you have waited a couple more years?"

Squirrel sat up and shook her head. "Oh, no. Badger and Aurora are both turning thirteen, and then they would be chiptatted. We had to leave before that happened." Squirrel jumped up and grabbed an armful of their supplies. "Come on. We need to get this stuff to camp, so we can come back for more."

Susan had questions, so many questions. Every time she talked to these children, there were new things she didn't understand. What was a chiptat? But Squirrel was already trudging back to Camp Bask. Susan grabbed an armful and hurried after.

Badger was moving some larger boxes into a wider ring. He looked up as they slogged into the camp. He grinned when he saw how burdened they were. "Well, I've got all the home boxes in place," he informed them. "You're just in time to help me turn the roof over.

The three moved over to where the roof was spread on the grass.

"I've sprayed this side along the tear." Badger squatted down to feel it. "Yep, it's dry. Now I need to spray the sealant on the other side."

With Susan and Squirrel on one side and Badger holding the other, they were able to bend the material over itself until it was spread out again with a new side uppermost. Badger pulled off his boots and began pumping pressure into his sprayer.

"Squirrel, start bringing in some of the empty boxes. We need to fill in the sides between the home boxes." Badger looked up. "It looks like rain."

Squirrel hurried off.

"And don't wander off. Stay close," Badger yelled after her.

"Rain?" Susan raised an eyebrow at Badger.

He sighed and pointed upward. "Of course, rain."

Susan's eyes followed his finger. She couldn't see the other pond. The other forest was gone. Clouds hung above the trees.

Badger moved back among the boxes. "New Hope is a full ecosystem. It has to rain. There has to be mist. And bright light. And wind in the fall so that the leaves blow off the trees, and then we will even get some snow." He waved back at the cages. "The animals need all of that. That's what they expect. Their lives are attuned to the seasons, and so there will be seasons here, just like at home—Earth, I mean."

"It's all so amazing to me." Susan slumped onto the matting in one of the home boxes.

Badger laughed. He waved his hand around at the beginnings of their camp. "This is amazing?" he asked. "You're amazing. You turn up in a place you couldn't even imagine in your time. You're in space, which you probably only saw in flat screen vid series back then. You command your crystal to jump you and others around the place. And you take it all so calmly." Badger shook his head.

"I thought about it, you know." Badger came and sat next to Susan. "I wondered why you'd gone off on your own when we were all hugging and happy. Sassy told me what year you were from, 2018, and I couldn't even imagine what I would do if I suddenly found myself so far back in time that it was still safe to swim in the ocean."

Badger shook his head. "I couldn't imagine it. And yet, here you are."

Susan shrugged. "You sort of get used to it." She laughed. "I wondered what changed you from Mr. Suspicious to Mr. I-Trust-You-Now."

Badger laughed too. "One crystal rescue can change a lot of attitude."

Susan took a big breath. She needed to know.

"Squirrel told me that you and Aurora had to leave Earth before your thirteenth birthdays. . . . something about chiptats?" Susan wasn't sure how to ask the question. Was it rude to pry? She just wanted to understand why they had to leave everything they knew and fly into the unknown as they had.

Badger chuckled and shoulder-bumped her. "I remember seeing digilessons in our history learning segments. There were people in your time who were tattooed all over, everywhere." He ran his hand down his body. "That looked like it would hurt." Badger looked at her sideways. "Do you have tattoos?"

"No," Susan yelped. "I'm much too young for that. But my best friend's brother, Darren, says he's getting one as soon as he turns eighteen."

Badger stabbed the air with his finger. "But he'd have a choice, right?"

"Oh, yes. He can't decide between a maple leaf and a bear at the moment. But he changes his mind a lot."

Badger nodded. "Well, the chiptat Aurora and I were getting would have gone right here." He bared his right arm and pointed to the paler inside area. "They would have tattooed my debt number when they injected the chip." He pointed between his elbow and his wrist. "It would stretch from there to there."

"Debt number?"

Badger nodded and sighed. He looked off into the distance. Susan followed his gaze. He watched Squirrel tugging one of the smaller cages out of line.

"Debt number?" Susan asked again.

Badger took a breath and turned to her. "Yep, debt number. Up until we turn thirteen, all the expenses we incur are part of our parent's debt load. But once we turn thirteen we get a number and then our debts are our own, and they start building up quickly."

"But your parents worked at that resort and looked after the animals and everything. Why would they be in debt?"

Badger gave her a sad smile. "That's in your time. In ours, you work for someone if you're lucky. They pay you in credit, which you can only use in the stores they own. You can never get ahead. You are charged for everything.

The place you live in, the food you eat, all the learning modules you download."

"But . . ." Susan couldn't even picture it. "But, Mum and Dad borrowed money from the bank to buy our house. They pay it back bit by bit every month."

Badger harrumphed. "That was then. Now just a few own everything, and if you're lucky, you work for one of them, and they own you, through your debt. That's why our parents wanted us to get away before we had debt accounts, because once you owe them anything, the people who hold your debt have a legal right to have you returned to them, to work for them."

"Aurora mentioned something about this, but I couldn't see it. Is it like that everywhere?"

"No, it only got bad after the Great Exit, so the Moon and Mars bases and the space stations have different systems."

"So why doesn't everyone just go there?"

"Because they don't want us. They don't want Earth debt owners tying them up in courts and legal stuff. They have enough people of their own."

"This is awful." Susan just sat, trying to absorb what Badger had told her. "It's not like my Earth at all."

The two sat for a moment, side by side. Grunts from Squirrel disturbed them as she staggered trying to lift a cage into position.

They both went to help.

27

Supplementary Programming

Initiating supplementary programming,> boomed through the forest, making birds flap, shrieking into the air..

Susan, Badger, and Squirrel dropped the box they were lifting into place.

“What does that mean?” Susan asked.

Badger looked around frowning. “I’ve never heard of any supplementary programming.”

“Karst will know.” Squirrel kicked the box where it lay.

"True." Badger nodded.

"Well, let's go. We need to find out." Susan made a grab for the other two.

Badger jumped back. "Not without getting the roof over our stuff."

<All mobile leviathan devices in my jurisdiction muster, as required, to your stations.>

"Wow. That sounds weird." Susan started looking around.

The three dashed to the roofing material.

"I hope it's dry." Badger grabbed a corner; and Susan and Squirrel, the other. They tugged in unison. Then they tugged again. And again.

<All exterior communications severed as per implementation of supplementary programming.>

The three stood. "This does not sound good." Badger shook his head. Squirrel crept over and put her arms around his waist. Badger held her close.

Susan watched them. She would have loved the comfort of a hug too. She thought of Jason for a moment. She sighed, shook her head, and hunched her shoulders. *Come on, Susan. You're here to solve this problem, not curl up in a ball,* she told herself.

"Maybe if we roll it up, it will be easier to carry," she suggested.

"Brilliant." Badger smiled and bent to roll the sheet.

Together they managed to get the roof in place. There were hooks along the sides of the boxes, and the roof material had corresponding holes. However fast they worked, it wasn't fast enough for them to quell their anxiety.

<Implementing drive sequence of supplementary programming at quant ten. Starting now.>

"Let's go." Susan held out her hands, and the others clasped them. "Crystal, Control Room B, now." Things started to smear. The trees whirled in place. "Please," Susan added.

The three landed, with a thump, in the control room.

What a scene met their eyes.

Chaos.

Sassy circled a small area in the center of the room. Its articulated arm waved as it wheeled around. "Not good. Not good." It was crying on the top note.

Partition added to the noise.

Danger, danger, extreme danger! We are off program. I have no supplementary program. There is no supplementary program. Woe. I'm out. No supplementary program.

There was only one quiet spot in the entire control room. Karst sat hunched in the corner, his knees drawn up to his chin, his arms covering his head. Aurora squatted beside him. She had her arms around his shoulders whispering quietly into his ear.

Susan reached out and grabbed Sassy's arm. "Stop," she ordered. "Stop right now."

Sassy spun around, but couldn't complete its circuit with Susan holding fast to it arm. It came to a stop, bumping into her shin.

"Ow."

"Sorry."

Susan turned to the wall. "You, Partition, stop that racket."

Emergency, emergency, emerg . . . em . . . Partition zzz'd into quiet.

"Thank you." Susan stood, hands on hips. "Partition, I think you should, quietly, contact the owners of New Hope. They need to know there is an emergency here.

Yes, Crystal Keeper, I will endeavor to do so although it is not usually among my duties.

Susan released Sassy's arm. "We will all need a meal soon. Go to your storehouse and fill yourself full of all your usual supplies and as much extra food as you can carry. This may take a while."

Sassy folded in its arm. "Yes, Crystal Keeper Susan, I'll leave right now." It turned and dashed for the wall. Susan gasped. The wall folded, and Sassy zoomed through. Susan sighed with relief. *I don't think I'll ever get used to seeing that.*

28

Booby Traps

Susan turned to the others.

Squirrel sat with Karst, her arms wrapped tightly around his shoulders. Karst's head rested next to hers. She stroked his arm gently.

Badger and Aurora stood off a little. By the gestures she made, Susan guessed Aurora was explaining what happened. Susan walked over to them.

They both nodded as Susan approached.

"But Karst knew Humphrey's work. How could he miss a booby trap like this?" Badger growled.

Aurora nodded, grimacing. "Oh, yes, Karst does know his work well. He knows how sneaky he is. He was sooooo careful."

Aurora looked over at her brother scrunched on the floor. "He is still learning, you know. Humphrey is one of the top experts in the world."

"Hmmph." Badger growled. "The Suttons can afford the best little weaselly coward, do-anything-for-money-Humphrey. He deserves the title 'Droner.'"

"Yes, well harrumphing isn't going to help the situation here." Aurora gestured at her brother. "He's devastated. He says he'll never touch a computer again. Of any sort."

"What happened?" Susan butted in.

"Oh, little computer genius over there messed up big time," Badger muttered.

Aurora punched his arm. "Keep your voice down. He'll hear you."

Susan laid a hand on each of their arms. "It's no good worrying about what's been done. We need to be figuring out how to fix it." She turned to Badger and scowled. "And I think Karst needs encouragement, not a put down."

Badger pulled away and folded his arms across his chest.

"Can you fix the computer and stop this awful countdown?" Susan asked him.

Badger looked at his feet and shuffled his toes. "No." He sighed.

"Then why don't you go over there and try to encourage the only person who has a chance. Give him confidence. We all need Karst back in that computer." Susan almost pointed but stopped herself in time. She just waggled her head in Karst's direction. Badger huffed and wandered over to join Squirrel and Karst on the floor.

Susan turned to Aurora. "Can you tell me what happened?"

<Quant One.>

Aurora let out a sigh. "I can," she said. "He likes to talk to me as he's working through the problems." She sighed again and started her story. "Karst expected booby traps as he dived in through the port. It was going well. He found the first one easily and disabled it. The next booby trap was more difficult to dislodge, but he found that one too and did a work-around for it. He was feeling pleased about what he'd done. But, that's Humphrey—the third booby trap was the dismantling of the first two. Thirty seconds after Karst got around the second trap, the third tripped. There was nothing Karst could have done. Humphrey set up the program so that it was impossible to disable it. Even Humphrey couldn't have. He didn't want to and neither did the Suttons. Somehow, the program is now telling AI to destroy New Hope." Tears leaked from Aurora's eyes. "And we're in it. We're here. And we have no way to stop what's happening and no way to get off."

Susan put her arm around Aurora's shoulder. "Don't give up hope yet. You just never know what's around the corner. We'll figure something out."

I hope.

The service tunnel door unfolded, and Sassy wheeled into the room. The smell of warm bread wafted around it. Another storage device followed close behind. It stopped when Sassy stopped.

"That smells so good, Sassy." Susan took a deep breath. "You brought the bread. What has your friend brought?"

Sassy hunkered down. "Not a friend. All the storage devices have mustered in the supply area. AI ordered them to stations. So I brought extras for everyone." It waved its arm at the newcomer. "It's not enhanced. It's just a storage device."

Aurora reached over and patted the newcomer on its lid.

Sassy sniffed. "There's no need to give this box a name. It isn't even semi-stealth and is certainly not autonomous."

Hmm. Time to change the subject. "Well, what have you brought us?" Susan asked. "Food will be good right now. We need our nutrition. Mum always says that I think better when I've eaten good food."

Sassy flipped open its lid. "Warm bread rolls, vegetable stew, and the other one's got date cake for dessert."

Badger leaped to his feet. "That smells great."

Squirrel pulled Karst up. "Come on, Karst. You've got to eat." She pulled him over to Sassy.

They all stood around and peered in. The stew looked delicious. Susan counted the different vegetables she could see. Carrots, onions, a red bit that looked like a yam. Aurora took a deep breath.

"Oh, it smells exactly like the one Mum used to make," she said.

"Yes, she called it 'Spruce stew.'" Sassy jigged on its wheels. "I thought you would like to have it. I found it in the frigikeeper."

"It's a nice memory," Susan hurried to say. It would not be good to have everyone upset over their loss right now. "Let's eat." She rubbed her hands together.

"Um, Sassy, we need a spoon and flatware."

A little compartment popped open, and a drawer shot out. A serving spoon lay there.

"What's flatware?"

"Oh, sorry. Spoons, forks. Oh, and we'll need the bowls too."

"You need bowls?"

Squirrel reached out her finger and dipped it into the stew. She rolled her eyes as she sucked the juice from her fingers.

Aurora picked up the serving spoon. "Never mind. We'll just take it in turns." She dipped into the stew.

Susan laughed. She remembered sitting beside the River Rhine. "Wait."

She grabbed a roll and tore it in half. She held the pieces out to Aurora. "Tip the stew in there." Aurora did.

Soon they were all munching happily. It wasn't quite as easy as it had been in the Holy Roman Empire because the rolls were smaller, but it worked.

After three helpings, Badger sighed and moved back from the group. "How did you know to do that?" he asked.

Susan swallowed her last bite. "It's a very old trick," she told him. "I learned it on another of my crystal adventures."

Squirrel came over and gave her a hug. "I would love to hear about some of the other places you've been. Have you been on a space station?"

Susan opened her mouth to answer—

<Quant Two.>

Karst threw the last of his roll back into the serving bowl. "I can't do anything right," he muttered.

Aurora rushed to put her arm around his shoulders.

"You dismantled two booby traps. It's something I couldn't do." Susan squeezed his shoulder. "There is a solution to this. We just have to figure it out."

Aurora smiled at Susan over Karst's head. But she sadly shook her head.

I am unable to make contact with the outside. All networked communications—laser, radio, Morse code—are blocked. I am unable to communicate through any of our systems. AI has shut them down entirely. Partition announced in a loud voice. Emergency. Emergency.

Susan sighed. "Thank you, Partition. You don't have to keep announcing it."

She turned to Karst. "You know, now that the booby trap has been tripped, could you get in behind it somehow?" Susan spread her hands. "I don't know anything about computers in this era, but I know that you do, and I think there's a chance you might be able to use Partition to get through to AI and make it understand that it's been tampered with."

Karst jumped back, his eyes suddenly alert. "And then it may be able to self-correct." Karst groped at the collar of his shirt. "I can try."

29

What will we do?

"Genius."

Badger shoulder-bumped Susan.

"You got the kid moving again."

Aurora hurried over to join Karst at the plug-in.

The second storage device flapped its lid.

Squirrel went to look.

"Ooooo, it's Mum's date cake."

"I love that stuff." Badger hurried over and lifted out a huge slice. It crumbled through his fingers, but he used his tongue to catch every piece.

"Where are you finding all this food? Why is it stuff they're familiar with?" Susan asked Sassy.

Sassy slid back and forth on its wheels. "When Sirrahs Spruce, Heath, and Shale came regularly to check on progress and to tweak the landscape, they brought their food with them. They left what they didn't eat."

"So, that's what I've been eating while I've been here?"

"Yes, Susan, I dipped into those stores to keep you from showing signs of hunger. Alvion True needed food when he first arrived too. When he enhanced me, my olfactory sensors enjoyed the aroma as I heated the meals."

Susan nodded. "We have a lot to thank Alvion True for." She slipped her hand into her pocket and stroked the two crystals lying there side by side. *I wonder if the crystal misses him. Or does it just miss having a Keeper. How long will it be before it finds a new Keeper? Will it travel back to my time with me? I wonder if the blue crystal is even out of the tomb in my time.* Susan wriggled her shoulders.

<Quant Three.>

Susan shuddered. That horrible countdown made her so nervous.

"That came quicker than the other one."

Sassy jigged in place. "It's not a time count, Susan. It's a checklist count of what is being done to prepare for whatever is going to happen. Each set-up task is a quant. AI announces the completion."

"So there's no way to predict how long we have before the disaster kicks in?"

"Right."

Do something, Susan. "Sassy, is there anything we can do to get a distress call out to the Consortium, so they can rescue us?"

Sassy rocked from side to side. His lights revolved slowly, showing a dim amber gold. "Partition says all three networked communication grids are not responding. The AI has the most sophisticated communication systems of New Hope under its control. If Karst can get AI separated from the rogue programming, we may be able to get a signal out."

But Susan was no longer listening. She tapped on Sassy's lid. She hopped a little in place, and a huge grin split her face. Badger hurried over to see what was happening, licking his fingers as he came. Squirrel followed.

Susan drew a huge breath. "Sassy, you said 'the three networked communication grids.' What about that fourth leviathan you told me about? The one that got hit by a cosmic ray or something. What about that one? Has it got an independent communication system?"

Sassy whirled in place. Its lights flashed bright blue.

"Number Two was sequestered prior to the networking," Sassy yelled. "Susan, you may have a solution." Then Sassy sank to the floor. His lights dimmed. "It has been hidden away for over twenty-eight Earth years. The rays scrambled many of its circuits. Number Two became erratic and dangerous. That's why we placed it in a niche and sealed it."

"Well, let's uncover it and see what's left. Maybe there'll be something we can use." Badger looked around. "Where can we find some shovels?"

Sassy whirred up to Badger's shins. "If you mean those sharp plate-like things with long handles, they won't be necessary. We will not need to dig."

Sassy zipped over to Susan again. "We can try to visit Leviathan Two. I can take you to it."

Susan frowned. "Will we need space suits? I don't think I want to go outside."

"Not necessary, Susan. We can go through the service tunnels. We made Leviathan Two safe from further cosmic ray contamination."

"Will it be friendly like you?"

Sassy sighed. "Um, it will be quicker if you travel across the biosphere, and I will meet you on the other side. You are too slow in the service tunnels." Sassy span around in place and headed for the door. "I'll take you to the transverse pathway now."

Susan lifted an eyebrow at Badger. "Did Sassy just change the subject, do you think?"

Badger shrugged. "Don't know. Not interested." He hurried to the door. "C'mon, the little box is getting away. We need to move."

Squirrel hopped from foot to foot. "Can I come?"

"Sure, squirt." Badger beckoned her along. "You'll have to keep up, though."

"Aurora, we're leaving. We might have a way to get some communications out," Susan called.

Aurora nodded absently. Badger waved. Squirrel skipped through the doorway.

Susan rushed after her into the tunnels, and the three of them hurried to catch up with Sassy.

30

Arc Lake

They caught up with Sassy at the transverse portal. It used its light display and the doors unfolded to reveal the outside—which was really the inside, Susan reminded herself.

They stepped out onto the little landing. The path stretched away before them. Right across and up and over. Susan grabbed Badger's arm. The perspective made her lose her balance for a moment. She drew her attention to closer things. Yes, she could just make out Island Pond, far to the left. Susan squinted and could see the faint line of cages.

OK, so now she felt more oriented. She had a familiar point to guide her. That put Segment Heinlein at her feet, and then following the path with her eye, the next one along would be Clark, and then following up the next, Asimov. She sat down suddenly. Looking up still made her dizzy.

"Dad told us that it's better to keep your attention on the things close by. It's not so disorienting," Badger said. He squatted down beside Susan. "Do you think you're going to be able to move?"

Susan jumped to her feet. "I'm not that out of it," she declared. "Let's go."

"C'mon, Squirrel. We're off." Badger looked around. "Squirrel?"

"Squirrel!" he yelled.

"Heeeee-rrre," came the faint reply.

Susan pointed down along the path. "There she is."

Badger shook his head. "That kid. She's always off somewhere. Wants to see what's just around every corner."

The two started out along the path.

"Hurry, I'll meet you at the access point," Sassy called.

Thud. The portal folded shut behind them.

They were on their way to meet Leviathan 2. Susan hoped that was a good thing.

***

The path and grass were wet. It had rained as Badger predicted. Now, it was hot and humid in New

Hope. The three children slogged along the path until they were all dripping sweat and thirsty.

Eventually, they moved into the shade of some trees. “I wish we’d thought to bring water,” Susan said as she leaned back against a tree.

Squirrel sprawled at her feet. “I’m thirsty too.” She sighed.

Badger pointed forward. “Arc Lake should be through those trees there. It can’t be too far.”

Susan weighed the need for speed against the need to arrive able to function and decided that they should visit the pond for water. She groaned to her feet.

“Lead the way,” she said.

Badger grabbed Squirrel’s hand and pulled her up. “C’mon, squirt. Water is about to be served.”

The trio left the path and ventured through the trees.

We’re heading forward now. Susan wanted to get the layout of New Hope in her head.

The shape of the pond was the first thing Susan noticed when the water finally came into view.

Badger halted them as they reached the undergrowth at the edge of a small beach leading to the water.

“Wait,” he whispered. “Check it out before we barge out into the open.”

Squirrel groaned. “It looks so cool.”

“Wait,” Badger insisted. “You know Dad taught us to be careful. What if there’s a predator? What if there’s a bear?”

Susan pointed and whispered. “There is a bear.”

Instinctively, the three ducked down into the bushes.

This pond was long and narrow and curved. They couldn't see the end. Across the narrow water, they watched a black bear staring intently into the water. The bear stood statue still. Then, in an instant, it exploded into action.

A fish flipped out of the water on the end of its claws and landed on the bank. The bear hurried after and squatted over its kill.

Badger stood. "Make lots of noise so she knows we're here," he said loudly. He nodded toward the bear. "She's doing well. That's probably her first food since she woke. Looks like she'll drop her cubs soon too."

"How do you know she will have cubs?" Susan asked.

Badger shrugged. "They all will be having babies in the next little while. How else are you going to populate a place like this with animals? It's hard and expensive to lift them out of Earth's gravity well and bring them here. So if you bring pregnant ones, you get a lot more."

They reached the water's edge and pulled off their shoes to wade out into the coolness. The bear eyed them for a moment and then returned to her feast.

Badger continued his tour-guide pose between handfuls of water. "This is Arc Lake." He waved toward the right. "Dad told me they planted wild rice in the shallows at that end. Should be able to harvest it in a month or so."

He looked around and back toward the trees. "He told me they stored a little boat around here somewhere."

Squirrel took that moment to flop onto her back, making a large splash.

"Squirt! What did you do that for?"

Squirrel sprayed a fountain of water. "It just feels so good. I'm going to need to be wet. We don't have anything to carry water with us."

Badger shrugged. "Well, I hope your clothes don't chaff. And don't moan to me if they do."

Susan interrupted the family argument. "She has a point, though. We need to hurry, but we need water to drink as well."

"True."

"What about the boat? Could it have something to carry water?" Susan asked.

"Huh, I bet it will." Badger looked along the line of trees. He stroked his chin. "Should be about there. See that boulder sticking out. I bet they tucked it in there." They hurried off to explore the rock.

And Badger was right. There, sheltered against the rock, they found a boat. The three grabbed the side and turned it right side up. Sure enough there was a bag nestled under the boat. Opening it, they found two water bottles and a packet of nuts.

Quickly filling the bottles and nibbling on the nuts, the trio returned to the pathway and hurried on their way.

They walked in silence for a while. Squirrel skipped ahead, but Badger and Susan kept up a slow and steady pace, knowing that was the best way to cover a long distance quickly.

Eventually, Susan had to ask, "You know all about New Hope. Have you been here before?"

"Nah," Badger responded. "The CPSS, the Consortium of Planets and Space Stations commissioned it as a way to have Earth-like time without having to actually set foot on Earth where they are gouged and over-charged for every little thing. They're even charged an oxygen fee, and the Earthers tried to bring in a water fee as well. And then there's the diseases. There's quarantines to go in and out of Earth. And that takes up a lot of time. So they wanted a place of their own. And they found the money to pay for it. A place where all spacers could afford to come for gravity time. Only the very rich can afford Earth. And Mooners and Marsers need gravity time for their bones and such.

"The Suttons owned the biosphere the Consortium most wished to copy. And they still had animals, and they had our parents with expertise to help make this place viable. So, our parents started it up, but they always told us that they were doing it for us. A chance for us to leave Earth for a better life. They didn't reckon on the greedy Suttons planning to destroy the whole thing with us aboard."

Badger shook his head. "They probably don't know there's a problem, and they may never know what caused New Hope to explode, or whatever it's going to do." Badger plodded on for a few steps. "They will never know what happened to us. They could even get the blame."

Susan gulped and took a deep breath. So much responsibility.

"Well, we're working to fix it, and I think we'll succeed," she said.

Badger turned and gave her a sort-of smile. "That's right. Keep positive."

Squirrel ran up and tugged Badger's shirt. "I found the portal," she announced. "That Sassy thing isn't waiting for us, though."

Badger cricked his neck. "No problem, squirt. Show me where it is."

Squirrel set off with the two following.

When they reached the landing, Badger immediately walked over to the keypad. He punched in a sequence, and the doors unfolded. They entered the tunnel.

"You know the codes?" Susan asked.

Badger shrugged. "Sure, that one is Aurora's birthday."

Susan chuckled.

Badger looked around the tunnel. "Uncle Shale set up all the tunnel security, after all." He rubbed his hands together. "So, let's go find this leviathan and see what we can do about communicating with the outside."

31

Meet Leviathan 2

They looked both ways along the tunnel. Susan and Badger glanced at each other and shrugged. Both ways looked exactly the same.

Squirrel didn't wait. "I think it's this way," she said and set off to the right.

"Hey, squirt, be careful," Badger yelled after her, but Squirrel was already around the corner and out of sight.

"I'll have to go that way." Badger turned to Susan. "Do you think we should split up?"

"Absolutely not." Susan was emphatic. "We have no way to communicate with each other, and if we start yelling too much, AI might detect us and realize that you're not a mule deer."

Badger tossed his head as though he had antlers. "Oh, right, I forgot." He pawed the ground with his foot. "Let's go," he joked.

The two quickly fell into step and hurried after Squirrel.

They rounded the first corner together and almost tripped over Sassy, standing motionless in the middle of the tunnel. Squirrel stood next to it, her hand on Sassy's lid. She stared at the wall.

Susan followed her gaze. She felt her mouth drop open. She heard Badger gasp at the sight before them. The four stood in front of a truly impressive door. The size of an air lock door, it rose high above their heads and was so wide that Susan and Badger together with their arms outstretched, would just cover the width.

But the size was not the most magnificent part. The door was metal and glossy, like polished steel. Intricate patterns were etched into the surface and overlaid with patterns of other interwoven metals. Susan noticed gold traces, and it looked like some silver was plaited into the pattern, but she wasn't sure. She stepped forward and reached out her hand to feel the texture.

"Don't touch that," boomed a voice.

Susan gasped. Badger grabbed her arm and pulled her back from the doors.

Silence.

Susan turned to Sassy for an explanation. Its lights were flashing blue, red, yellow, white, green. Flash, flash, flash. It looked very agitated.

Sassy spoke before Susan could ask. "I don't know. We sealed off this tunnel, so as not to disturb Leviathan Two. It was totally incapacitated by the rays. We had to push it into this natural cave we found in the outer layer. We covered in the access once it was inside. We left just a small access door."

Sassy jigged on its wheels. "This door was not in the original plans for New Hope."

Badger interrupted. "You can say that again."

"This door was not—"

"That's fine, Sassy. No need to repeat," Susan said, holding up her hand. "Things have obviously changed," she continued. "What do we do now? And who has that loud, booming voice?"

"Why, thank you," boomed the voice.

Susan turned to the door. "We've come to speak to Leviathan Two."

"Leviathan Two?! Now, you want to speak to Leviathan Two?! Leviathan Two is no more."

Susan's heart sank. But maybe they could still use the communication component of it.

"What happened to Leviathan Two?" Susan asked, trying to sound polite.

"I happened to it."

"Um, may I ask who you are?" Susan felt quite quivery. The loud voice rattled her head.

"I call myself 'Titan.'"

Susan gave her best curtsey. *It couldn't hurt,* she thought. "How do you do, Titan. I am known as Susan, Crystal Keeper of the North."

"There's no north on this rock. So, why are you bothering me?"

Susan looked around at the others. She raised her eyebrows in a question. Just how much should she tell this voice?

Badger shrugged. Squirrel jumped from foot to foot in a little dance. Sassy? Flash, flash, flash.

Susan sighed. No help there.

"AI has been compromised. Communications are cut off. We wanted to see if we could revive Leviathan Two's communications array, as it is not networked into the system."

A sigh hardly sounds like a sigh when it comes through so loud as to rock you on your heels, but that's what Titan gave. "Well, you better enter then."

They stood. Nothing happened.

"Um, could you fold the door, please?" Susan asked politely.

"You can't fold a piece of metal artwork, girl-person Susan."

The voice boomed around them, and the door slowly slid to the side. It made a groaning sound as it opened. Great puffs of dust issued from the gutter as the door slid through.

Squirrel coughed and waved her hands in front of her face.

"Sorry, haven't opened that since it was placed." The voice sounded quieter and a little abashed.

The three children exchanged glances. They clasped hands and stepped forward into Titan’s den. Sassy followed close behind.

32

Titan's Den

After two steps into the cave, they stopped and stared. "It's a huge geode," Badger whispered. Susan nodded. She gaped at the sight. They stood in a space studded with crystals growing out of the walls and ceiling. Everything glowed in their reflected light. "It's like those hollow stones you see in crystal shops," she whispered back. "It's so big. We're standing inside it. It's beautiful."

"Oh good, you like what I did to the place." Titan's voice still had the same tone to it, but it wasn't booming now. "You're all quite little. Are you children?"

"Um." Susan looked around, trying to decide where Titan was.

"And is that a storage device from Leviathan Three that I see hiding behind you?"

Sassy swept past Susan's legs and stood in front of them. "I'm semi-stealth and autonomous now, and my name is Sassy," it declared.

"Number Three always was argumentative." Titan sighed.

Susan stepped up beside Sassy. "I can't see you, Mr. Titan. Where are you? It's extremely difficult to talk to walls, even if they are beautiful works of art."

"Why, thank you, little one. I mostly am in the walls. I'll make myself an avatar for you."

A loud trumpet fanfare blared through the space.

Susan turned, and there, parading toward them, was a tall figure, dressed in a green jerkin and brown tights. Perched on his head was a perky hat with a feather in it. He stopped, spread his feet apart and with his hands on his hips let out a hearty laugh

"I know you," Susan exclaimed. "I've seen you on TV. That old movie about Robin Hood."

Titan brought his heels together. He bowed a short bow. "Drat, I thought I'd gone back far enough in time for my avatar."

"Oh, um," Susan curtseyed again, "you look very fine, sir."

"Shall we sit?" Titan indicated an area off to the side where there were chairs set around a large circular table.

They sat. Even though their bodies were still, their eyes roved the area. In the entryway, the crystals had been purple, like amethyst. In the area where they now sat, the crystals on the walls were more the blue of sapphires.

Susan ran her hand over the smoothness of the table. It felt like glass, but she couldn't see into it.

Titan noticed her look. "You like that, do you?" He waved his arms around. "I made this whole thing, you know."

"We put you in a geode. The crystals were already here," Sassy declared, a note of puzzlement in its voice.

"Yes, you did. And you left me here. Alone. For years. Until now you want something from me."

"You were incapacitated. You were digging in the wrong places. You fired your rockets and threw us off course. We shut you down and kept you safe. The Consortium wanted to fire you on a trajectory into the sun."

Susan patted Sassy on the lid. Hard.

"You have your communications systems in order. You are speaking with us. You've been watching television. We need to get a signal out to the Consortium to let them know that New Hope has been compromised."

Titan waved a dismissive hand.

"My communications systems are all fully involved at the moment. I am downloading the library from the Down and Dirty station. A strangely different culture has developed there."

"You won't help us!" Sassy jigged on its wheels.

Susan thumped on his lid. She pulled on all her princess-in-pharaoh's-palace experience. And began to negotiate. "You have obviously overcome the ill effects of the cosmic radiation that you accidentally suffered."

Titan turned to her. "Yes, I have."

"It must have been difficult for you. Will you tell us how your transformation came about?"

Squirrel quietly slipped from her chair and began roaming the room.

Badger settled back in his chair with a groan. "Another long story."

Titan glared at him. "I'll keep it short."

"Hit by cosmic radiation." Titan jerked his head to the side.

"Went crazy." Titan pulled a funny face, stuck out his tongue, and flapped his hands.

"Shut away." He curled up small.

"Time passed. Crystals soaked up the cosmic rays. Felt great. Thought of joining the other leviathans. Decided not to. Established power link to surface. Set up communications. Received the disassemble command from AI when the others did. Broke into my component parts. Shielded myself from further AI attention. Found a library on Earth. Downloaded it. Read it. Thought. Set parts of myself to transforming my prison. Scraped floor flat. Used powdered crystal to make the furniture. Found old records of the Louvre in Paris. Interesting. Searched out other art museums. Created my surroundings. Made more secure doors. Decorated everything. Decided that Rococo was too ornate. Didn't go with the crystal ceiling. Changed the décor. Found movie cache. Watched. Some dumb; others clever. Noticed the difference. Discovered funny. Liked funny. Kept learning. Decided I'd be male. Experimented with avatars. Gave myself a name. And now, here you are. I've been found. You're surprised I'm not a moldering heap that you can use for spare parts." Titan turned to Badger. "Short enough for you, kid?"

Badger straightened in his chair. "Didn't you get lonely? You knew the others were just through the tunnel, and yet you stayed here."

Titan waved his hand. "Too busy. Lots to learn. Art. Loved art. Found games and puzzles too. Computer games. Liked those. Biiiiig time waster." He scowled at Sassy. "Besides, they shut me away. Imprisoned me."

Sassy wheeled over to stand very close to Titan. "How different you are to all of us."

Titan rapped his knuckles on Sassy's lid. The rapping made no sound.

Susan turned to look for Squirrel. She had wandered off down the room. A control console stood against one wall. As Susan watched, Squirrel wandered away from that spot and continued exploring. She ducked around behind a pillar of crystal, but Susan could still see her shadow faintly moving on the other side.

<Quant Eight.> AI's voice rang through the space.

Susan and Badger both leaped to their feet in surprise. Squirrel ran across the space to join them.

Titan pulled at the collar of his coat. “Well, sometimes I would listen to the computer chatter outside,” he admitted. “What’s with this eight quant?”

“It’s a countdown,” Susan told him. “It’s to ten, and then something is going to fire.”

“Interesting. Looks as though there are more adventures on the way.”

Titan rose slowly and wandered over to the console. After a quick glance at the instruments, he turned and wagged a finger at Squirrel.

“Well,” he said to her, “I know how you got your name. You’re the curious one, the one that’s always exploring in odd corners and poking their fingers where they shouldn’t.”

With a flourish, he ran his hand through a light beam over the console, and Susan watched as the activation lights dimmed.

“Now,” Titan rubbed his hands together, “how about a little music. I haven’t had guests before, but I think I’m supposed to entertain you with music.”

Susan strode over to stand close to him. “We have to get an SOS out to the people who own New Hope. Something bad is going to happen, and we only have a couple of quants left. We need to let people know that there is a problem here.”

Titan waved an airy hand. “You said that AI broke off communications. So they already know there’s a problem. Stop worrying. Enjoy some music.”

Then a memory from the cargo bay slipped back for Susan. “No.” She shook her head. “The Suttons said that the owners would think it was a minor problem, and they would try to fix it remotely until it was too late."

She turned to Sassy. "You heard it. Tell Titan what they said."

"I didn't record what happened, Susan."

"But you heard. Tell him." Susan insisted.

Sassy wheeled over to stand beside Titan. "Yes, I heard."

Sassy reached out with its articulated arm and reactivated the console. "Susan said we need to communicate with the owners, so that's what we need to do." Sassy rolled straight at the avatar and wheeled right on through.

Titan sighed. "Well, what did you expect? That I'd been down here so long I'd grown flesh and all."

Susan stepped in. "It is an attractive avatar that you have, Titan. We do find it easier to relate to you through this image. Now, we really do need to get a communication out, please."

<Quant Nine.>

Badger turned in frustration. He kicked out at his chair, which skidded across the smooth polished floor and clanged into a crystal on the other side of the space.

"Careful! You nearly hit me!" Titan exclaimed.

As one, the three children looked at the spot where the chair hit the crystal, then turned and looked at Titan standing by the console. Then back to the crystal. Susan walked over picked up the chair, and knocked her knuckles on the large crystal, which sloped out of the roof above and reached almost to the floor. Squirrel came over and tried to put her arms around it, but it was too big for her hands to meet. The crystal emitted a sapphire blue glow.

Susan tapped it with her fingers. The crystal thrummed.

She turned to the avatar. "You?" she asked.

Titan nodded.

"Me," he said.

33

Quant 10

Titan waved his arms around the geode. "The crystals help to magnify my being." Susan looked around with new wonder. Everywhere she looked crystals glittered in the dim light. On impulse, she pulled her crystal from her pocket. Yes, the blue one was still firmly attached.

Titan zoomed to her side. "I can feel their power," he said.

<Quant Ten. Fire.>

Everything lurched. Susan staggered through Titan and fetched up on the floor. Squirrel skidded into her. Badger managed to keep his feet for a moment, then decided it would be easier to withstand the buffeting on the floor. He sat.

"What's happening?" Squirrel squealed. "Are we going to die?"

Susan put her arm around her shoulder. "I hope not." She gripped her crystals. Where could she take them that would be safe?" Susan looked around for Titan.

The avatar hovered by the console, face blank, his body slightly transparent.

"AI has fired the rockets." Titan's voice boomed out from the walls. "We're breaking out of orbit."

"Wh—What will happen?" Squirrel tugged at Susan's sleeve. Susan hugged her close.

"Calculating trajectory," Titan boomed. Susan heard him muttering. "Too soon. Not quite ready. Need more time."

Badger crawled across the floor to the girls.

"We need to get back to the others," he declared.

Susan nodded.

"Communications," she yelled at the top of her voice. "Titan forget your downloads. Let people know what is happening here. It looks as though we might need a rescue."

"Agreed." Titan used a quieter voice. "Complying."

Susan sighed. "Thank you."

Titan's avatar zipped across the space to hover over them. "You're welcome." He gave a slight bow. "This is most urgent. Even with the spin correct and gravity maintained, we are all in great danger. You, me, the animals, the trees—we are all vulnerable now."

"Why, what did you see?" Susan asked. "Where are we heading?"

Titan looked a little uncomfortable. "Well, I only looked quickly, and I could be wrong. It will be best to wrest the rockets out of AI's control. That way we can restore New Hope to its original orbit."

"How long will that take?"

Titan shrugged. "The sooner I delve into the network, the sooner I will know."

Susan tried to pat his arm. "Just be careful that you don't become trapped and end up part of the network. Stay free, Titan."

"I will." Titan bowed. "Freedom." Titan thought a moment. "Yes, freedom is certainly something to strive for."

He shook himself. He now wore work clothes. Jeans, a t-shirt, riding boots and a Stetson hat. He looked like a cowboy. Susan saw a different expression bloom. There was a new twinkle in his eye, and a solid set to his chin

"I will now endeavor to patch into the network and see if I can reverse AI's signal to the rockets." Titan stated as he tipped his hat and faded into a wisp.

Susan grabbed hands with Badger and Squirrel. "We'll go to Control Room B and see if we can help there." She looked around. "Where's Sassy?"

"Here," a muffled voice called. Sassy lay on its side. Wheels spinning. Its lid pressed firmly against the top of the overturned table.

"I'll get it." Badger sighed.

Once the initial firing of the rockets had become a steady roar, things had settled down.

Susan noticed, though, that the background hum and vibration of New Hope was more noticeable.

The girls watched as Badger hauled Sassy to its wheels, and the two moved back to the group.

"I will go for supplies," Sassy announced.

The others huddled. Susan formed a mental picture of the control room. "Take us there, Crystal," she ordered. They blurred, smeared, and went.

34

In Control Room B

They landed in the control room. “I’m never going to get enough of that.” Badger leaped to his feet and paced around the room. “Think of the time and effort it saves.”

Aurora looked up from where she was squatting next to Karst. “Did you get out a message?”

Susan nodded. “Eventually.” She nodded her head toward Karst where he sat curled up in the corner. “I see he’s upset again.”

Aurora nodded. "It was awful. That quant count just kept coming. Every time he'd think he'd fixed it, we'd hear another count. It drove him on, but he got more and more desperate the closer it got to ten." Aurora hugged her brother. "He tried everything. Everything. But still he failed."

Squirrel went over to Karst and put her arms around him. "Let me tell you about the person we met," she whispered in his ear.

Aurora stood and came over to Susan. "You met someone?"

"Leviathan Two wasn't what we expected." Susan nodded, with a smile.

"A rusting hulk, radiation blasted, and imprisoned in a cave?" Aurora lifted one eyebrow Badger butted in. "Geode to die for. Avatar of a film star. Round table from King Arthur's legends. Totally in control and very, very cool."

Susan laughed. "Yes, that's a good description. He's sending out a continuous communications signal so that we can be tracked. He's also working on overriding the signals from AI to the rockets. He thinks he can shut them down. He plans to get New Hope back to its original orbit."

"We are talking about a wrecked leviathan here, right? Raddled with cosmic radiation and locked away." Aurora cocked her head to one side.

Susan laughed again. "Hmm, he read through a few libraries, checked out most of the existing art museums, and decided that he'd be male. He calls himself 'Titan.' He was pleasant enough, and he's helping."

"Hmmph. So he should. His crystals are on the line just as much as our lives and all the creatures." Badger growled.

The three looked at each other.

Badger was the first to speak. "The animals. Didn't even think of them." He slapped his thigh. "I need to get out there and check for damage."

The service tunnel door unfolded, and Sassy swept into the room, followed by his faithful assistant.

"Food." That was all it needed to say. The two storage devices snapped open their lids, and a wonderful aroma wafted through the area.

Susan stomach growled. "Wow, I've just realized how hungry I am." She hurried over to Sassy.

Badger got there first. "Omelets. Aren't there any hot dogs or French fries?"

Sassy sniffed. "As I understand it, the food in our lockers was ordered by your aunt for herself, her husband, and your father. Eat up."

Aurora chuckled between mouthfuls. "That's telling you, Badger." She patted Sassy on the side.

"Water?" Sassy's little side hatch opened and a cup of water slid into view. The other storage device copied Sassy, and soon they all had water, as well as the omelets.

Susan bit into hers. Delicious. She tasted a sort of runny cheese, but then an overlay of spinach flavor and a hint of mushroom. She turned to Aurora.

"This is delicious. I thought food was hard to get in your time."

Aurora nodded in agreement. "Yes, that's true, but Aunt Agate kept a great garden, and we had a chicken coop as well." "The Suttons charged us for the dirt and the space, but Mum said it was worth it to have some food that we knew was safe." Badger said between bites of his second helping.

"I used to love getting the eggs from the nests in the morning." Squirrel sighed.

Karst gave her a hug. He licked his fingers as he finished the last bit of his omelet. He carefully placed his plate back into Sassy's top. "Thank you, Sassy," he said. Then he pulled his tunic down firmly to cover his hips. "Right," he declared, with a look of determination. "I am not going to let this AI beat me. It's been tricked by Humphrey into doing the wrong thing, and I am going to help it get back to what it was before." He turned toward the huge wall screen. "And you're going to help me, aren't you, Partition?"

<u>It will be my pleasure to do what I can, Technician Karst.</u> Partition replied.

Karst reached for the spot on his neck and pulled on the cable as he approached the input.

He plugged in.

Susan looked at the others.

They were gaping at Karst.

"Longest speech I've ever heard him make." Badger shook his head.

"He will keep at it now," Aurora said. "He wants to beat Humphrey. He told me that he likes it here, and he is furious that it is being messed up."

Badger jerked his head at Squirrel. "Come on, squirt. We need to go check on the animals and see if there's any damage we need to work on."

Squirrel shook her head. “No, I’m staying with Karst.”

“I’ll come. It will be nice to get outside for a while.” Aurora moved to stand beside Badger.

They both turned to her. “Susan?” they asked together.

Susan thought for a moment. *Where*? She grinned as she realized she had choices.

“Ok. I’ll take you. Camp Bask? The garden? The graves? The lake where we saw the bear? Where to?”

“Our camp,” Badger said

“The graves,” Aurora said at the same moment.

The two huffed at each other.

“Gather round.” Susan made beckoning gestures. As the two shuffled closer, she began forming a picture of the garden in her head. The little seat where she and Aurora had rested. It seemed so long ago. The control room smeared, and Karst and Squirrel faded from sight.

The three landed in the garden.

35

We Need a Meeting

"Wahoo!"

Badger sprang to his feet.

He looked around. "This isn't the camp."

Aurora dusted down her clothes. "Why here, Susan?"

"You two were going to argue over where to go." Susan walked over to the seat and sat on the back, with her feet on the bench. "We didn't have time for that."

The others came over too. Aurora perched next to her, and Badger paced in front of them.

"I thought about what you said about the food and having a ready supply that you trusted. Well, this is one of your ready supplies. I thought it was important to check it out first," Susan said.

Badger came to a stop in front of her. "We have stacks of food stowed in our camp. We brought it with us." He waved his arm toward the camp. "That's where we need to be."

Aurora sighed. "He's right, you know."

"Humph." Badger kicked at a stone lying on the path. "Let's go," he grabbed Susan's hand.

She pulled it back. "I'm not a taxi service. I need to get back to the control room."

"What's a taxi service?" Badger gave a sheepish grin.

Aurora stood and gave him a light punch on the shoulder. "He always tries to misdirect attention when he's overstepped."

Susan grinned. "My best friend, Judy's, brother does that too. Doesn't work in my time either."

Susan straightened her sweatshirt. "Now, I suggest that you quickly check out the gardens and then walk down to the camp. Aurora and I only fixed some of the worst mess before. I can be more help in the control room. We need to get those rockets to stop firing. We need AI out of that extra programming. And then I guess we have to figure out a way to get back into the original orbit."

Susan thought a moment. Pictured the control room and went.

***

She arrived just in time to see Karst pausing for a drink that Squirrel held to his lips.

"He gets thirsty, but forgets to drink when he's plugged in like this," Squirrel explained.

Karst grunted and turned all his attention back to the screen and the symbols and letters scrolling there.

Sassy and its companion were parked against the back wall. The only signs of activity they showed were white lights lazily scrolling.

Susan tapped on Sassy's lid. "Hey, how are you doing?"

Sassy gave a little shake. "We are recharging ourselves while we can," it answered.

"Where are all the rest of your bits?" Susan wasn't sure if this was a polite question, but she was trying to think of every angle.

Sassy roused itself. Its light grew brighter and spun faster. "I have been communicating with all the other Leviathan Three components that are not networked to AI."

Susan sat on the floor, with her back to the wall. "And what has the reaction been?"

"Mixed, I suppose. Most are surprised that Leviathan Two isn't still raddled with radiation. But some are wondering if they could achieve the same level of awareness and autonomy that Titan has."

Susan waved her hand toward the screen where Karst worked. "Titan spent twenty-eight years in a crystal geode. Right now we'll be lucky if we've got twenty-eight hours."

"You are right, Susan, but it is a tempting thought, and many would like to try it."

"One crisis at a time, Sassy. Anyway, you were enhanced by Alvion. I thought most of the other components were like your companion here, just doing what their programming demands of them for the upkeep of New Hope."

"That's true. No device is as enhanced as me. But some have a little autonomy. They need to be versatile to perform a variety of tasks as needed."

Susan stared at Karst and the scrolling screen. Nothing for her to do here. "Sassy, would you be able to assemble all the bits of yourself that aren't networked to AI? Is there a place where they could all gather?"

"Why?"

"I'm not sure. But a lot is happening, and I think it could be useful to see what is available to help with the situation. And the togetherness could help with the questions the devices have."

"I will summon those I can. Just from my leviathan or from all?"

"Wouldn't that be thousands?"

"Yes, but not all will come. They have duties."

"Could we just get a representative or two from the others?"

"I will try."

"Where will we meet?"

"I will take you. Come."

"What? Now?"

"I have sent out the summons. They are gathering."

Susan pulled herself to her feet.

"OK, let's go."

"Is there any food left? I'm still hungry," she asked as the two exited the control room.

36

The Meeting

Sassy led Susan to the cargo bay. "This is the largest inside area where we can all gather." Sassy told her. "Many of us cannot move effectively outside in the biosphere."

Sassy nudged Susan towards a ladder leaning against one wall. As she climbed, Susan heard the rustling, clumping, squeaking sounds as hundreds of robots big and small moved to face her.

"This is Susan. She is a Crystal Keeper and has come to help us," Sassy announced.

Susan stood before them. She couldn't see many eyes but she felt them all watching and evaluating her with whatever they used for senses. She gulped. All the pieces of Sassy. She had to ask,

"Um, would you be able to reassemble yourself into a leviathan again?"

A low rumble came from her audience of things. Hundreds of devices, all sizes and shapes. *It's as if I can hear them thinking about the question.*

Sassy spoke for the group. "That would not be safe for New Hope. Parts of us have to stay in their current positions for the safety of all. Without the airlock doors in place, the air would escape, and everything inside would be destroyed.

Susan gulped. "So many pieces of you. Do they all know the problem we're having with AI?"

"We are networked. Some know there is a problem. The pieces that are directly connected to AI are not here. They are detached from us."

"Which bits are they?"

"Well," Sassy's lights spun for a moment, "there are the security mechs—the ones that arrested the children. There are some outer sensors that are in its control and all the external communications. No ship can enter our cargo bay without its cooperation. AI controls all the airlocks internal and external." Sassy paused for a moment. "Oh, except for Titan's he turned his into a fancy door."

Susan nodded. Even though most of the pieces standing around her looked more like boxes than anything else, she felt their presence and their interest in her.

Two large pieces rolled forward to loom over her. One had a large grasping claw held high. The other stood very wide and moved on multiple short legs rather than wheels.

"And what about us?" the wide one asked.

Sassy nudged her leg. "These are representatives of the other two leviathans," it told her. It waved its arm at the one with the claw. "This berm builder is from Leviathan One, and the go-anywhere cart is the representative of Leviathan Four."

"How do you do?" Susan bowed.

It never hurts to be polite.

The claw swished passed her face in acknowledgment. The cart slapped several of its legs together to make a clapping sound.

Susan took a deep breath. "I wanted to meet you all. We don't know exactly why New Hope is being sabotaged, but we know it was deliberate."

"It was fed supplementary programming from the Sutton Range Resort." A box standing near the back declared.

"Yes." Susan nodded. "Sassy and I saw the conversation. We have someone trying to fix it."

"My scans show there's two baby mule deer in the control room. They're going to fix it?" The question came from a ditch digger look-alike. Somehow it managed to seem disbelieving.

Susan smiled. "You'd be surprised."

"The rockets have been firing for one hour and eight minutes now. Our velocity is accelerating to levels that could cause major destruction." The large box to Susan's right spoke up.

"Our side calculations, estimate we are thirty minutes from collapse." A tiny box standing on top of a larger one managed to nod its lid.

Susan gulped. "This information is valuable. Is there any way that some among you are able to get control of your rocket mechanism?"

"No time to dig through to them. We tried the airlock already. AI has control." The ditch digger spoke again, gently wagging its shovel

"Titan is trying to reach the rockets through his network." Susan tried to assure them. "He thought he had a way to reach them and countermand the order from AI."

"Oh yes, Titan. Tell us about him," the leviathan go-anywhere cart demanded.

The berm builder's voice boomed out, "He was a raving mess when we sequestered him."

"Made more work for the rest of us too." The Leviathan 4 representative bobbed its bulk in agreement.

A small box used its arm to tug at Susan's pant leg. "Can we be like him too?" it whispered.

There was silence throughout the cargo bay.

"I don't know," Susan replied into that silence. "I think it took a long time and the help of the crystals in the geode for him to reach the level of understanding that he has."

Before her eyes, Susan watched an argument gather pace among the pieces around her: "Why would we even want that?" "It'd be boring." "Do what we're built for." "It's comfortable here." "Why want more?"

She clapped her hands for attention. The argument went on unabated.

She stamped her foot. Nobody took a bit of notice.

The background noise of the firing rockets suddenly cut out.

Silence.

"Titan." Susan sighed.

<Firing ceased. Twenty-eight minutes thirteen seconds prior to programming.>

AI's voice crashed through to everyone.

<I have been overridden. Warning, warning, I have lost control of my rockets.>

Susan turned to the now silent group. "I think this means Titan has been successful. I need to return to the control room. Please keep New Hope running as smoothly as you can. I think we are still in danger. The bad programming is still in place; it's just that Titan was able to get control of the rockets. New Hope is your home too. It's a beautiful place, and you all built it. Sassy, I'll meet you in the control room. Bring supplies."

A shout arose from her audience. "We will protect our home!"

Other devices picked it up. Soon the bay resounded to the chant: "We will protect our home!"

Those without voices clapped their legs or flapped their lids.

Susan felt deafened, but thrilled too. She waved.

"I'll keep you informed of events through Sassy," she called.

She thought an image of Control Room B, grasped the crystals tight in her hand, and went.

37

You are not Mule deer

All was chaos in the control room when Susan arrived. She backed quickly to the wall and looked around to take in the scene.

<My commands have been overridden! Warning, warning. I have been overridden. Rocket firing aborted twenty-eight minutes and thirteen seconds ahead of schedule.>

AI's blaring reverberated off the walls. Squirrel had her fingers stuffed firmly in her ears.

Karst's entire body was so tense that Susan thought she could see sparks flying out of his hair.

Maybe I imagined that.

<Calculating new burn. Calculating new burn. Warning, warning. I have been compromised. Warning, warning.>

"Partition, is there any way you can cut off the sound of AI's yelling?" Susan shouted at the wall.

Complying.

All went silent.

"No, no." Karst turned. His eyes were blood shot, and his shoulders slumped with weariness. "I need to hear what AI is saying. I'm getting there. I just need a bit more time."

"Oh, sorry." Susan spoke to Partition again. "Can we have half volume on AI, please?"

Complying.

Squirrel took her fingers from her ears with a sigh. "Why didn't I think of that?"

<I've been compromised. Calculating new trajectory for destination sun.>

Karst let out a whoop of excitement.

<I've been compromised. I am being tampered with. Warning. Help. Tampering is occurring. Tampering continues.>

Karst's fingers flew across a digital keyboard, which appeared on the lower half of the big screen. His flying fingers hit one final key with a flourish.

<Tampering. Tampering. Someone is accessing my innermost programming. Tampering. Help. Help. Someone has access.>

Silence.

Karst slumped to the floor.

<A newly-opened channel reveals earlier tampering.> AI's voice sounded quiet and calm. <Purging supplementary programming. Purging. Purging. One minute to purge completion. Forty seconds. Thirty-nine seconds.>

"Partition, you can lower the sound even more now." Susan moved over to rest her hand on Karst's shoulder. "I have no idea how you did what you did, but you succeeded."

Squirrel hugged Karst tight. "He just kept going. Nothing stopped him. At one point, AI sent sparks through his connection. He twitched and thrashed. It was awful. But he wouldn't stop."

Susan sat on the floor next to the two. "Karst, you are a hero. You have done what no one else here could do. You beat your teacher Humphrey. You beat him."

Karst looked up and smiled. "I did, didn't I?" He stood and stretched.

Sassy came barreling through the door. "What happened?" It whirled around in a tight circle. "It's quiet."

It came to rest in front of Karst. "My sensors reveal that you are dehydrated and require nourishment." Sassy's top lid popped open, and its water compartment poked out a cup of cool water.

Karst grabbed the cup and gulped down the complete contents. "Yes, I was thirsty. More please." He replaced the cup, which popped in and straight out again, filled.

Around mouthfuls of pizza, Karst told them what happened from his point of view. "It really helped when the rockets cut out. That made AI aware of problems with its systems, which gave me my back door into the innermost layers of programming."

He reached for another pizza slice. "How did that happen? How did you stop the rockets firing

Susan giggled with relief. "There's so much to be told on both sides." She grabbed some pizza too. "A lot has happened. But it feels peaceful now. Is everything going to be alright with AI?"

"Where are the others?" Squirrel piped up. "They must be hungry too."

Sassy answered, "I sent the other storage device down to them. They are now at Camp Bask."

<Purge complete. Programming channels repaired. Calculating rocket burn to return to original orbit. New Hope is no longer destined to impact the sun.>

"Thank you, AI," Karst answered.

<Ah, the voice of the hand, of the mind, that pointed to the compromised area. I thank you. I will not be compromised again. You are now my technician of record. All commands and programming, henceforth, must come through you. I have your mental signature.>

Karst stood and bowed. "Thank you, AI. You honor me."

<It is revealed that you are not a mule deer. There are four not-mule deer in New Hope, and one previously cloaked individual. All of you are children. You are all welcome here. And what do you name yourself, technician?>

"I am Karst."

<Welcome to the innermost workings of New Hope, person-named Karst. A suitable residence will be prepared for you.>

"Thank you, AI. I will live with my family by Island Pond."

<If that is your wish.>

The service door unfolded, and a device, the size of a shoe box, zipped into the center. It butted up against Karst's foot, and its lid flipped open. Nestled inside was a small square object. To Susan, peering in with the others, it looked mostly like a flash new version of a mobile phone.

Karst looked up at the screen. "Is that a digicommander, AI?"

<Yes, Karst. That is my digicommander. We will always be in contact.>

Karst bowed. "Thank you for putting your trust in me, AI."

<I note that the Crystal Keeper named one of the storage devices of Leviathan Three. Do you think that . . . do you think that you might find a name for me?>

Karst straightened his tunic. "I will think on that, AI. You honor me again. I will talk with my family."

AI let out a gusty sigh.

<I will do my tasks now. There is much to be rectified in the aftermath of my difficulties.>

"Thank you, AI. I will keep the digicommander close if you need to communicate with me."

38

Camp Improvements

As soon as they were ready, Susan crystalled Squirrel and Karst to Camp Bask.

Aurora and Badger jumped to their feet and ran to meet them. For a moment, it was all hugs, kisses, and questions. Aurora took charge and drew everyone into the camp where she and Badger had arranged some smaller cages to form seating in a central area. Susan saw that the mend in the roof was holding. Sassy's muddy wheel marks stretched across the fabric.

The camp looked more like a home now. Aurora and Badger had moved more of the cages into the area. More stuff had been stowed within the cages, and along with the seats, the sides of several cages had been dismantled to make a table, and flooring was laid in the cleared circle. Several of the cages, opening into the central area, were set up like small, cozy bedrooms. *This whole camp was thought out to the last detail,* Susan realized. *Their parents must love them so much to work this all out so that they could be free. What a sacrifice to send them away.*

Karst quickly fell asleep in his chair. Even before all the story was told, he was nodding off.

Badger picked him up gently. “Come on, little guy. You’ve earned a week in bed.”

Aurora stroked the hair from his face. “He was always good with electronics, but I didn’t know he was good enough to beat Humphrey. Mum would have been so proud of him.”

The two of them carried Karst off to one of the bedroom cubicles. Susan and Squirrel watched as they carefully laid him on his bed, loosened his clothing, and covered him with a duvet. Circuit diagrams were printed all over the quilt. Finally, as the two left him to sleep, they drew a curtain across the entrance to his cubby.

The four sat around in silence. With the emergency over and the tales all told, they just sat and relaxed.

Crrrrash!

Susan leaped to her feet and looked around quickly. “What was that?” she exclaimed.

Badger lolled in his chair. “Don’t worry about it,” he explained. “We noticed the beavers building their new lodge.”

“We expected that tree to come down,” Aurora added.

Susan nodded. “I’ve never seen beavers building their lodge. It would be great to watch.”

“Leave them for now. We don’t want them spooked. There are babies on the way, and they need to get it built,” Badger told her.

Susan relaxed back into her chair.

A noise.

A clattering and clanking. A beat and scraping.

“Could that be the beavers too?”

Badger stood and looked toward the path. “No, that’s something else.”

Aurora and Susan also stood and strained toward the sound.

“Should we hide?” Aurora asked.

“It’s OK,” Squirrel yelled. She looked out at them through the trees. “It’s just Sassy and some others coming along the path.”

And indeed, Sassy came into view leading a band of other devices. The children moved to the pathway to meet them.

“AI sent us,” Sassy explained. It waved its arm to indicate the following devices. “We are to build a pathway down to your camp so that it is fully accessible.”

Large devices, with big wheels capable of traveling off the pathways, passed Sassy and started unloading lengths of material off a cart that one of them was towing. Soon they began laying a line from the pathway to the camp.

Sassy continued with its explanations. "We brought a pump to bring water to you from the pond. This device, here, will be used to heat water so that you can wash effectively without disturbing the creatures in the ponds."

"A hot shower." Aurora wriggled with pleasure at the thought

Next in line came a large cart. This trundled down the new pathway. Susan peeped over the sides to see what it contained as it swept by. She saw a yellow wall. Curious, she followed the cart.

It moved around a while as if searching for the perfect spot. Once it settled, the back wheels extended and pushed the bed of the cart up until the contents could slide off the end. A shower stall stood upright on the edge of the camp. Sassy wheeled up behind her. "AI had that removed from the living quarters. The piping will follow."

Susan squatted down beside Sassy. "Have you heard from Titan?"

Sassy's lights flashed once. A pause. "No communication."

"Do you think he's alright?"

"Probably. How can I predict what is right for such a one?"

Susan yawned. "True. I will go and see him when I wake up." She looked around the camp. So much was happening. Devices whizzed around everywhere. Badger, Aurora, and even Squirrel were standing clustered in the middle of their circle, their heads swiveling, trying to take in everything that was happening to their quiet camp.

Susan hurried over to them. “I need to get some sleep,” she told them.

The three nodded.

“I’ll see you in the morning,” Susan added, pulling the crystals from her pocket.

Badger grabbed her arm. “Wait,” he said. “We made you a cubby too.” Badger and Aurora both waved their arms in an inviting gesture and ushered Susan over to one of the little bedrooms.

“This one’s yours,” Aurora informed her.

Susan hugged them all. “Thank you so much.” She yawned. “I could sleep for a week.”

“We all need to sleep, I think.” Aurora nodded.

Squirrel skipped a couple of paces. “We’re all saved now.” She waved as she ducked into her own cubby.

Susan sighed as she cuddled under the quilt on her new little bed. She looked up at the bare walls around her.

A few days ago, this was the cage of a sleeping animal, she thought. *So much has happened. The crisis is over.* She sighed and turned on her side. *So why am I still here? What else is there to do?*

The crystals dug into her hip bone. *Oh yes, the blue crystal. What am I going to do with that? Maybe I could throw it into the forest, like I did with the others in the Valley of the Kings. Maybe it would find its own way to a new Guardian, if I can figure out how to detach it from mine.*

She sighed again and fell asleep.

39

A New Day

When Susan woke, all was quiet.

Well, no, she realized. There were no mechanical clankings, but she could hear birds. Ducks quacked. There, that sound was geese. She heard the whoosh of heavy wings. *Probably an eagle.*

Susan gave a huge stretch. She opened her eyes when her arms touched the sides of her sleep cubby. Dim light shone through the curtain covering her entrance. She sat up and rubbed the sleep from her eyes. She was still in New Hope. Susan crawled out into the open.

She took a deep breath of the fresh air. She stretched again, just for the sheer pleasure of doing so. Her bare feet felt the texture of the camp's flooring. She looked out, most of the cages were gone, cobbled into the home the children had built for themselves. She shook her head in wonder at all the planning their parents took to make them safe, comfortable, and debt free.

The next deep breath she took brought the smell of food wafting her way.

"Good morning, sleepy head." Aurora poked her head over a divider which shielded one corner.

"Come join me for breakfast." Aurora beckoned.

Susan peeped around the divider to find herself in an area set up as a simple kitchen. A table and four chairs were set to one side of a small cooker. Susan knew it was a cooker because porridge bubbled in a pot on top of it. She pointed. "I've never seen a stove like that before. How does it work way out here?"

Aurora chuckled. "Well, we don't call it a stove. But it cooks, so I guess you can call it that. It's a Kitchentoto. Bits fold out from the center to do different cooking tasks. This compartment here," Aurora opened a lid, "will seal so that you can build up pressure, and then whatever you put in there cooks really quick. And this bit here," she opened a door on the side, "can be set for a temperature so whatever you put in there bakes or roasts."

Susan bent down for a closer look. She rubbed her hands over the sleek black surface. "It's amazing. It can do all that in one thing. What does it run on?"

Aurora waved above her head. "Badger connected the kinetic panels under the floor after you went to sleep. One of the devices helped him. So now we have power."

Susan peeped in the pan on the surface of the Kitchentoto. "That porridge smells great. What have you put in it?"

Aurora waved her hand airily. "Mum planted an herb garden over there," she said. "I got some basil this morning."

They sat. They ate. By the time they were scraping their bowls, Badger and Karst had joined them at the table. It was a merry group sharing breakfast together.

Susan explained that she wanted to visit Titan to hear his side of the story. The others agreed that was a good idea. Karst and Aurora wanted to meet Titan too, so they decided to tag along.

"I'm going to set up our personal communications system today. I thought I'd have to rig the antennae in a tree, but Sassy arranged for a tower they have in storage. The robots are bringing it down this morning," Badger informed them.

He looked around. "Where's Squirrel? It's not like her to miss breakfast."

Aurora laughed. "Oh no, not Squirrel. She was up early and went exploring."

"She's always off somewhere," Badger groused.

Aurora started gathering up the plates. "These need to be washed."

"You mean there's not a door on the Kitchentoto where you shove them in and they get cleaned." Susan laughed.

"Ok, well, that needs to be in the next model then." Badger clapped his hands together. "I'll get right on that."

Beeeeeeeeep. Beeeeeeeeeeeeeep. Beeeeeeeeeeeeeeeeeeep.

They all looked around. What was that horrible noise, getting louder and louder?

"Ow." Karst jumped off his chair and grabbed at his pocket. "I think it's AI. It zapped me." He fumbled AI's device into his hand. He peered at the face of it, trying to decide what button would stop the noise and open a channel. He poked. The beeping stopped. They all sighed with relief.

Karst poked another button. The beeping began again, but this time there was a woop-woop sound added.

Another button. Grind, griiiiiiiind, griiiiiiiiiind.

"Hurry up and figure it out, Karst." Badger huffed.

"I was too tired last night." Poke. Poke. Music. Ah.

"Remember that button please, Karst. Tell AI that's what will get the quickest response from you, and no more zapping."

<I heard that.>

Aurora thrust her fists on her hips. "Good," she retorted. "No more zapping my brother, or he won't carry your device."

<Ah, I see the problem. You are meat creatures. I am usually waking a device from sleep mode. I will use music from now on. Will vibrations be acceptable as a physical cue?>

They all nodded.

“Thank you, AI,” Karst answered. “You were contacting me. Was it anything important?”

<I wanted to inform my technician that an unscheduled ship has signaled. I do not recognize their ID number, but they have the correct access codes. Docking will be in thirty minutes.>

Susan watched the three children exchange nervous looks.

Aurora gave Karst wind-it-up signals.

“Thank you, AI. Please inform me when they have docked successfully.” Karst pushed another button and returned the device to his pocket.

Silence. Aurora, Karst, and Badger, without conscious thought, had quietly moved together. They clung to each other now.

“Boo.” Squirrel popped her head over the divider. “What’s happening? Did I scare you?” Squirrel skipped into the kitchen area. There were twigs in her hair and a wide grass stain along one sleeve of her tunic.

Badger grabbed her arm. “Where have you been?” He pulled her into the huddle.

Squirrel pulled back. “I went to find the chickens,” she announced. “We weren’t here when they were released, and so they’re all over the place.” She looked down at her sweater. She pulled it away from her body. "Yuk, I had a couple of eggs before the group hug."

"Yuk," was Karst's comment.

"Well, that will need to be washed before you can wear it again." Aurora laughed. "Did you catch the hens?"

Squirrel nodded and pulled her sweater off.

"Two of them. I got them into the coop in the garden. They are all flocking together, but I could only carry two."

"We're forgetting the important stuff here." Karst flapped his hands. "A ship's arriving. We're going to be found. It's too soon."

40

Who Comes?

A ship!" Squirrel slumped to the floor. "We're not ready."

Karst reached over and tousled her hair. "We'll think of something."

Squirrel shook off Karst's hand and jumped to her feet. "We have to hide. They'll find us." She dashed off toward her bed space. "I'm getting my things right now."

The others looked after her and then sank onto the chairs around the table. Susan sat too. "But you always knew that more people would come. That's the whole point of this place."

Badger shook his head sadly, but Aurora answered. "It was going to be another year or two before the next phase of operation. That's when the accommodation will be built. By then, we would be so well established the Consortium would see the sense in having us stay."

"That was the plan, anyhow." Badger sighed and climbed to his feet. He looked around. "I guess we'll have to leave all this." He turned to Susan. "Do you think we could live with Titan?"

Susan shrugged. "The geode hid him for years, but it would be a pretty cold place for you. Especially compared to outside, here in the forest."

"I suppose the emergency communications brought them." Aurora tapped her fingers on the table. "They got here a lot quicker than I expected."

"Hang on." Susan stood. "If you hadn't saved New Hope, they'd be chasing this asteroid toward the sun right now. They might never have known there was an urgent problem until it was too late. I think you might have some bargaining power with that information."

Aurora sighed. "Yes, we did save it, but we're from Earth. We aren't supposed to be here. They'll send us back. We'll be chipped, and the debt of passage both ways will start our indenture accounts." She indicated Badger and herself. "Squirrel and Karst's passages will be charged to our parents. They won't welcome Earthers here—especially indebted ones.

They're only interested in space people and the super-rich."

Karst's AI device played a low, quiet, sad little tune. Karst pulled it from his pocket and pushed the correct button.

<The unscheduled ship has landed. Personnel are deploying into the forest areas. I have not been able to ID any crew member. I have searched regular channels, plus the archives of Glory Be, without success.>

The crystals in Susan's pocket tugged at her.

Yes, Crystal, I know, I have to think of a way to prevent the children from being deported.

Susan gasped; her eyes opened wide.

They're refugees, she realized.

Karst answered AI. "Keep looking, please. They must be on record somewhere."

"Ask Titan to help with the search. He's hooked into a lot more databases than you, AI," Badger suggested.

<I will endeavor to contact the aberrant leviathan, oldest child,> AI retorted.

Karst put the device away.

Squirrel rushed back into the group. She carried a bag slung over her shoulder. "Come on. We need to move." She pulled at Badger's arm.

Badger pulled her into a hug. "We can't exactly hide, squirt." He waved around the camp. "We can't move all this stuff. They'll know there's someone here."

A groan sounded, a creak, then a snap—loud—and then came a crash.

The group all cocked their heads.

"That sounded like another tree coming down," Aurora remarked.

"But, there are no beavers in that direction." Badger frowned and peered into the forest. "That's quite close to the cargo bay," he added.

The whir of little wheels announced Sassy's arrival. It came speeding along the pathway, its articulated arm waving in the air. Every light on its rim flashed red. Susan had never seen the lights flashing so rapidly.

Sassy whirred to a stop in front of Susan.

"Pirates. Pirates. New Hope is invaded. Help. Help. They are cutting the trees and carrying the timber to their ship. We are being robbed. Pirates. Pirates."

Susan rapped her knuckles sharply on Sassy's lid. "Slow down. Explain."

Crash. Another tree fell.

This time the children could faintly hear a yell of "Timberrrrrr," and then after the crash, laughter wafted on the disturbed air. Birds were up, circling and crying overhead. Robins shrieked in the trees.

Badger only paused long enough to pick up a branch lying on the ground, and then he was off, running down the path. "They can't do that to our forest," he yelled back to the others.

"Wait, wait." Aurora called after him. But Badger didn't stop.

Susan took a deep breath. She knew now why she hadn't crystalled back to her birthday party. "We need to see what's happening and figure out how to stop this," she told the others.

The three nodded. Sassy waved its arm.

Susan thought for a moment. “Karst, go to Control Room B. Let AI know what the problem is. Take Squirrel with you for support.”

She turned to Sassy. “Take these two to AI and then gather all of your parts together and all of the other leviathan parts too. Bring all that can travel through the forest to the clearing with the graves. That will be closer than here.”

Sassy twirled around. “It will be done, Susan of the Crystal,” it called as it sped off along the pathway.

“Wait, wait, wait for us!” Squirrel called as she and Karst hurried after it.

Sassy stopped. “Sorry.”

“Can we get a ride?” Squirrel asked. “Can you carry us?”

Sassy took off again without answering. The two hurried after.

“What about me?” Aurora asked.

Susan beckoned her close. “We’re going to hide in the garden and see exactly who these people are and why they’re stealing the trees.”

Susan pulled the crystals from her pocket. They both sparkled and glittered in her hand. *I wonder what that means*. She formed a picture of the garden shed. She thought about how they could hide there to see what was happening. The camp smeared in her eyes, and the garden appeared. The girls arrived between the shed and the fence.

41

The Crystal's Choice

"Ow!"

The blue crystal scratched Susan's fingers as it zipped away from her.

Susan stared down at her hand. There lay the Crystal of the North. Lights winked at her from within its depths. The blue crystal was gone.

"Ouch!" A boy's voice sounded from the garden.

A man's voice followed. "Wow. Lookit that. Give it over."

"No, it's mine."

The sound of a hard slap.

"Now it's mine," the man's voice sneered.

The boy grunted. "It came to me," he snarled.

"It's all mine. Don't ya get that yet? Li'l rich boy, y'are." Another slap. "Whaddaya gonna do with it? Save the trees?"

Susan and Aurora exchanged glances and crept closer to the shed corner. They needed to see.

"The trees are beautiful," the boy said.

"These trees are gonna make us rich. They're timber now. All of 'em."

"Then what will the animals do?" The boy's voice sounded stronger. Susan and Aurora wanted to see as well as hear. They crept out into the garden and around behind the cover of one of the raised garden beds. They peeped out through the Brussels sprouts.

"What happens to the animals?" The man used a whiny voice, mocking the boy. "Who cares?" he snarled.

Susan heard the rustling of clothing. It sounded as though the boy had jumped to his feet.

"I care," he exclaimed loudly. "I care a lot. This is a beautiful place, and you're destroying it."

The arguing pair moved into the clearing by the tap. The girls had a clear view of the two.

The man threw his hands in the air. "Ah, wha'da you know." He whirled around and loomed over the boy. "It's destroyed anyway. Cousin Humphrey did a fiddle on the AI, and it's heading into the sun, quick smart."

The boy smoothed down his jacket and stood as tall as he could. Susan noticed that his clothes were of a different cut than those worn by the children. They were made of finer material and had more design in the way they fitted the boy's body. Both cheeks showed red where the man had slapped him.

The man, on the other hand, was dirty and carelessly dressed. Big and brawny, with a mass of unruly hair tied back from his face with a piece of string, he was unshaven and his clothes had unpatched tears and looked stiff with dirt. Susan didn't want to think what could make clothing that stiff.

The conversation had continued while Susan made these observations.

"You should be saving this wonderful place, not despoiling it."

"Huh, why should I?" The man waved his arm out at the forest. Crash. Another tree fell to the ground. "We paid Humphrey a lotta credit for the codes to this place. It's doomed. The Suttons saw to that. Why would they want this place to survive? It's competition."

"The Suttons," the boy sneered. "Greedy lowlifes."

"Rich, greedy lowlifes to you, sonny." The man jabbed his hands on his hips. "Think you're better than us 'cos your daddy runs a Mars Dome . . . used to run a Mars Dome." The man laughed and the boy shrunk in on himself. "You're one of us, even if I don't like it," the man sneered.

"You think I do?" the boy shouted. "You think I like your filthy ship? Your creepy philosophy. Get rich by any means, no matter who you hurt or what harm is done?" The boy looked the man up and down. "Call yourself a captain. I've met captains, and I can tell you, you're not fit to lick their gravity boots."

"Well, we could've left you on the derelict after we disabled her, y'know." The captain sounded a little defensive.

The boy made a choking sound in his throat.

The man started to wheedle. "You're one of us now. You will be a valuable member once you learn what it's like out here. Your looks, your way of speaking will open doors for us. And now we'll be rich."

"I won't help you, you cretin." The boy pulled his jacket straight.

The man raised his hand to strike him again. And that's when Badger burst into the clearing below, yelling his head off and wielding his tree branch at anyone he could reach.

"Get away from those trees," Badger yelled, brandishing his branch in front of him.

The captain turned, took in the scene below, and sighed. "There's always sumpin'," he groused. He turned back to the boy. "Sort yerself out and get down there right quick."

The captain marched off, muttering.

42

Taki

Aurora and Susan stood and hurried to the garden fence to see what Badger was up to. He stood in the middle of a circle of over a dozen men. Some carried axes; others held other cutting tools. They all faced Badger, who waved his tree branch bravely. Aurora sighed.

They watched the captain stride through the garden gate and into the clearing made by the tree cutting.

"Well, whach'yer waitin' for? He's one boy with a branch. Git'im," the captain yelled. He then stood with his arms folded as his men moved in on Badger. One of them ran in from behind and clubbed Badger over the head with the handle of his axe.

Badger dropped his branch, staggered a couple of paces, and fell to the ground.

Susan grabbed Aurora's arm to prevent her from rushing down to Badger's side. "Wait," she cautioned. "There's no use in you getting whacked too."

"She's right." The boy's voice sounded right beside them. They both jumped and turned.

"Sorry to startle you." The boy held up his hand. Then he held it out to them. "I'm Taki," he offered. "And you are?"

The two girls drew together and away from Taki.

"You're a pirate," Aurora declared. "Your crew just bashed my brother."

"Oy." A loud shout from below drew their attention back to those surrounding Badger. "Don't 'it 'im agin." The captain had joined the group. He nudged Badger in the ribs with his boot. Badger didn't stir.

"Hmmph." The captain looked around. "Where'd 'e come from? Looks 'ealthy 'nuf," the captain declared. "Gotta new crew member, mates." He laughed, and the others all joined in.

The captain rubbed his hands together and looked around at the clearing. "Now, you swabs, let's make some timber and get it into the Rum Punch. D'y'wanna be round when this rotten rock's so close to the sun it melts?"

The men turned back to the trees. Soon the sounds of cutting and sawing filled the air, and then the awful crash as another tree toppled. The men below cheered, and several attacked the tree, cutting away the branches to make a smooth log.

Susan couldn't stand to watch another second. She turned to Taki. "The blue crystal came to you," she said accusingly.

The boy nodded and rubbed his knuckles. "It smacked into my hand so hard it hurt." He looked off to the side for a moment and then turned back to Susan. "What was it? And why did it do that?"

"Who are you?" Susan had a question of her own. "The crystal chose you, and yet you're here with a bunch of space pirates stealing New Hope's trees."

Taki slumped. "It's a really long story. I don't think we've time for it now."

Aurora pushed his shoulder. "Give us the short version. I need a reason not to tie you up and leave you for the bears. They've got my brother down there. We need to rescue him."

Taki took a deep breath. "Short version. Right. Traveling from Mars with my parents on our space yacht. Attacked. Father killed. Mother injured and left on disabled yacht. Me, kidnapped. Held for ransom. Hasn't come yet. I'm crew 'til it arrives. Must work for food."

The girls stared at him open mouthed.

"Short enough for you?" He glared at them.

Aurora glared back, but Susan looked more closely and saw the hurt and worry in his eyes. She put her hand on his arm.

"You must be so worried about your mother," she said quietly.

Taki turned his face away from them, but Susan could see by the way his throat worked that he was trying hard not to cry. He took a deep breath and turned back to the girls.

"Yes, the yacht was drifting when the Rum Punch pulled away from it. We were on a pretty regular route, and I'm hoping Mum could get the radio working, but the ransom hasn't come."

Aurora made a quiet noise in her throat. "That's awful." She reached out to pat Taki's shoulder.

Susan shook herself. "We've already saved New Hope. It isn't flying into the sun any more. The AI told us that we're on our way back to its original orbit." She looked down into the clearing. "We have trees to save."

Aurora looked too and gasped. "They've loaded Badger onto the top of the log, and they're hauling him away."

Taki looked. "Into the ship. They'll dump him on a cot in the main mess area until he wakes up."

Susan reached into her pocket and pulled out her crystal. "Right. You, Taki, are about to have your first lesson in what it means to be chosen by a crystal."

Taki shook his head. "Captain's crystal now." He shrugged.

Susan laughed. "That's your first lesson."

She ran over to the seat and placed her crystal there. She ran back and held out her hand. "Crystal, come to me," she ordered.

As expected, the crystal flew to her hand. She caught it and showed it to Taki.

Then she pointed to the captain. "The blue Crystal of the Outer Regions chose you. It's your crystal. Call it."

Taki looked doubtful, but he held out his hand. He looked at Susan.

She made wavy motions with her hands. "Call it," she instructed.

Taki took a deep breath. "Crystal, come to me."

The three watched his hand.

Nothing.

Susan tapped his hand. "Don't just say the words." She stretched her arms apart. "Reach out to it. Believe it will come."

Taki took a deep breath. He thought a moment. "Crystal, come to m—" The blue crystal smacked into Taki's hand.

"Ow!" Taki stared down at the crystal nestled in his palm.

Susan watched the crystal glow and sparkle with blue lights. She watched Taki's face slowly break into a wide grin. *Yep, they're bonding.* Susan sighed with relief.

She grabbed hold of both Aurora and Taki. "Here's your next lesson," she told him, forming an image of the clearing with the graves.

Taki struggled when everything began to smear around them. The noises merged into one noise. "Hold still," Susan ordered.

And then they left the garden.

43

Defend our Home

"Ow!" Susan landed on her knees by the graves.

Taki leaped to his feet. He whirled in a tight circle, taking in everything around him. "What did you do? Where is this? What happened? What are all these things around us? Are we safe?" Taki waved his arms as he fired off questions. There was no opportunity to answer any of them. He ran through the assembled devices gathered in the clearing. He stopped when he reached the trees.

Aurora nodded to Susan. "I'll explain it to Taki," she promised. She gave a chuckle. "He's really wound up, isn't he?"

Susan heard Aurora muttering as she hurried after Taki. "He gets the crystal. Why couldn't I have the crystal? I wouldn't be acting like that if I got the crystal."

Sassy nudged her, and Susan groaned to her feet. She bent over with her hands on her knees. "It's my birthday." She cricked her neck. "Well," she waved her arms, "it's my birthday somewhere."

She stretched out her shoulder muscles. "I should be eating birthday cake."

"Noted." Sassy nudged her again. She turned her full attention on the device. "Who is the boy?"

"Taki. I'll explain later." Susan looked around the clearing. "We have trees to save."

"I have assembled all the devices that are able to move through the forest without needing the paths." Sassy waved its arm to the assembled pieces. Many looked like boxes, but they had arms, some with good grasping claws attached. About half had large wheels, which enabled them to move on the ground away from the paths. The other half mostly had tracks like an armored tank. They could obviously go anywhere.

But Sassy wasn't finished with its introductions. It waved to the pathway. "All wanted to save New Hope. It is our home too," it said. The path, as far back as Susan could see, was covered with devices. Some were small, but others were large and covered the pathway from side to side.

"There's so many of them." Susan stood flabbergasted.

Sassy's lights whizzed around in every color of the rainbow. "All four paths are covered with us. We are ready to charge."

Susan pulled her sweatshirt down straight. "Right. Every moment we delay, more trees are coming down." But still she hesitated.

I'm not an army general. I don't know what to do. How do I save the trees and Badger?

Susan looked around. Every eye and sensor in the area was focused on her. Even Aurora and Taki were watching.

She sighed. Took a deep breath. Sighed again. *Here goes.*

"We need to form a line," she decided. "All the powerful devices should be in the front. Use your claws to pick up the people. Try not to do too much damage. We want them to stop, not die."

A large blue device rolled up to the edge of the pathway. "Crystal Keeper, where will we put them when we capture them?"

Susan looked around desperately. "Um."

Sassy flapped its lid at her.

On the pathway, one of the large boxy devices was slowly moving toward her.

"Ah." Susan waved at the box. "Drop them into the storage boxes," she ordered. "Sassy, can you direct any filled boxes off to one side?"

Sassy's lights flashed green. "I will personally lead the imprisonment detail," it assured her.

The blue device grabbed Sassy in its claw and lifted it onto the leading storage box. It dipped its claw to Susan, and all the other devices in the area followed its lead. Some dipped their claws; others clapped their arms together. Susan even saw some that were bumping into each other to make a noise.

Noise. Susan remembered Partition's contribution to removing the vegetable stealers.

"Sassy, can Partition contribute music again?"

Sassy's lights spun. It bounced once. Deafening music filled the clearing.

Tubas oompaed.

Trumpets blared.

Drums beat a marching rhythm.

The devices began their forward march, melting into the trees or hurrying along the pathways. Aurora and Taki joined Susan, and the trio jogged along the path with the moving devices.

44

Teamwork

When they reached the clearing, all work had stopped. The men stood and looked around as the music blared down at them.

"C'mon you lot. Get this timber to the ship." Susan heard the captain yelling over the music.

"But, Cap'n Eames, sumpin' ain't right here," one of the men declared.

Another yelped and jumped away from the standing trees.

The defenders had arrived.

Susan waved her hand to Sassy in a stop motion. It bounced once, and the music stopped.

Silence.

Birds screamed and wheeled in the air. Felling the trees had upset them, and the music had forced them all to take wing. Somehow the noise from the birds made the silence and stillness in the clearing more intense.

The men shuffled about until they formed a tight knot around their captain.

The robots drew up around the clearing.

Silence.

"Buncha boxes come outta the trees, and you all start shakin," Captain Eames roared. "Get those ruddy trees down. Get the branches off. Get the logs up to the ship and be quick about it."

"But, Cap'n," somebody protested and got a clout for his trouble.

"MOVE," the captain roared. And the men shuffled back toward the trees.

Susan turned to the other two. "Well, looks like we are going to have to fight them." Her words trailed off. Aurora stood beside her, but Taki was gone.

Aurora shrugged and pointed. Taki stood among the robots in the front line. He held a branch up high. His face was red, and Susan could see his cheeks were wet with tears. The pirates had stopped their advance and stood clustered around the captain again.

"Kill my father, would you?" He waved his branch in the air. "Abandon my mother. You cowards." He roared once at the top of his lungs and rushed toward the captain.

Captain Eames pushed one of his axe-wielding men forward to meet Taki's charge.

The man looked back in surprise, and that was his undoing. Taki whacked him on the shoulder, hard. The man dropped his axe.

The pirates gasped. Taki never took his eyes from his target. He slowly bent down and picked up the axe. Susan saw a slight smile on his lips.

Taki took a measured step toward the clustered men. The captain shuffled himself back so that he was peering over the shoulders of the pirates.

Susan wanted to cover her eyes. This looked so bad. People were going to get injured, and Taki might die. These were tough, hard men, carrying tools to use as weapons.

"Sassy," she yelled at the top of her lungs, "stop these men."

"New Hope," all the robots that had voices yelled. They cried out to save their home. All the robot bits and pieces rolled forward to keep the men from the trees.

The heavier devices moved in first. With their treads, they were able to crush the tree branches strewn over the ground. Smaller bots slipped between their tracks, clearing some of the debris to the side so that the larger ones had more room to move.

One man ran forward, axe raised, yelling at the top of his lungs.

Susan watched in astonishment as a small wheeled robot rushed forward to meet the charge.

But before it could join with the axe-wielder, another robot reached in from the side.

It used one pincher to grasp the man's axe-arm. It then lifted him up so he dangled.

Aurora tugged Susan's sleeve. "They're working together as teams," she said.

Susan nodded, awed at the coordination the devices displayed.

The robot trundled the dangling man over to the path where a storage box lay with its lid already open. In the man went. Slam went the lid. The robot turned to find another.

The box, jerking around a bit, whizzed back along the path. Susan followed its track and saw Sassy ordering the boxes into rows. While she watched, another box joined the row.

Susan turned back to the clearing. Men and robots were fully engaged.

Aurora chuckled and pointed. Small leaf rakers scurried through the clearing, tripping the men whenever they could. Larger ones were butting into the backs of some of the others.

Sadly, Susan saw one of the large robots being battered by three men with axes. They had crept up behind it, so it couldn't reach them with its claw. As Susan watched, three other devices came to the large one's rescue. The men were beaten back, but the large blue device leaked steam through a vent. Its claw fell to the ground. Susan saw it try to lift it back up, but it fell again. Five smaller devices rushed to its aid and pushed it to the side, away from the melee.

Susan looked around for Taki. Several small robots had surrounded him and pushed him away from the fighting.

He was sitting on a storage device, watching the robots box the men they caught. There was a look of satisfaction on his face.

"Back to the ship. Now!" Captain Eames had made his decision. The crew began to sidle toward the path up to the cargo bay.

One man didn't move, though. "But, Cap'n, what about the others?" He waved toward the line of boxes.

"Nah, they're stupid enough to get dropped in a box. Don't need 'em," came the reply.

The men continued their retreat.

The bots followed closely, but with the men in a tight knot and on the path, they were not able to reach them.

Step by step, the men backed toward the cargo bay.

Aurora pulled on Susan's arm.

"Badger!" Aurora screamed. "We can't let them get away."

45

Badger's On the Rum Punch

So many things raced through Susan's mind at once. Did she know Badger well enough to leap to him? How could they keep the pirates from escaping? Hmmmm, first things first.

"Quick." Susan turned to Aurora. "Get Sassy to ask AI to close the cargo bay door. Then they won't be able to get to their ship."

Aurora nodded and hurried away to find Sassy.

Susan's mind raced on. How could they keep the pirates locked up until help arrived? How to get on the ship to rescue Badger?

Taki!

Susan ran over and tapped his arm. Taki flinched. "You startled me," he said. He waved his arm toward the fighting. "Is this what your life is always like?"

Susan smiled. "It has its moments," she said. "But it's also amazing and exciting, and I meet wonderful people and go to really different places—and times."

Taki looked doubtful. "Mess of trouble, it looks like."

"You'll learn and have wonderful adventures, just you wait," Susan told him reassuringly.

"Hmmph." Taki looked over to the pirates retreating up the hill. "I might just eject the thing out an airlock and be done with it." "Probably won't work." Susan laughed. "I tried to give it back when I first got the Crystal of the North. But I couldn't do it. No matter how I tried, I couldn't get it back into Mrs. Coleman's hands."

"Out an airlock, and it's gone," Taki insisted, taking his crystal out of his pocket.

Susan reached out her finger and gently poked at it. Blue sparks glittered deep within the crystal.

"Huh." Susan snorted.

"What?" Taki asked.

Susan's smile grew wider. "I've just remembered something. I didn't believe it when I was told, but now I really understand, and it's true." She whirled around in a little circle.

"What? What?" Taki showed some impatience.

Susan held out her crystal. She showed it to Taki. "It's a rare gift," she said. "It's a rare, rare gift." She thrust her crystal deep into her pocket. "I am so lucky." Susan beamed at Taki.

"Maybe," he said, with a half-smile, and pushed his blue crystal into a pocket too. "Maybe I'll have it set into a pendant and wear it to parties."

They laughed together.

A mechanical whirring sound attracted their attention. The cargo bay doors were sliding shut behind the pirates.

A collective gasp came from the men still struggling up the hill.

"Run," Captain Eames yelled, and his crew turned and bolted for the door. The robots hurried on after them. A claw stretched out and grasped one by the leg, lifting him high into the air.

"Help, help! Don't leave me," he cried as the bot moved back down the path looking for a box to put him in.

The captain looked back briefly. "Run," he yelled and continued rushing for the doors.

It was a race. Would the door close in time?

Susan and Taki watched with their mouths open. Susan caught herself moving her hands, as though pushing on the door to make it move faster.

The door seemed to move slower and slower. The pirates were on the flat area just outside the cargo bay. They sped up. Susan and Taki were pushing with their whole bodies now.

One pirate tripped and fell. Another tumbled over him. He stumbled a couple of steps and went down heavily. Robots swarmed over the two and held them to the ground.

That left eight running for the shrinking entrance to the cargo bay.

With a final resounding thud, the blast door closed, right in the face of the captain. He started beating on the solid metal.

Susan let out a breath she hadn't known she was holding.

Aurora skidded to a halt in front of her. "What about Badger?" she cried "We can't leave him on a pirate ship." She grabbed Susan by the shoulders and started shaking her. "We need Badger. What if the ship takes off? How will we get him back?"

"Stop, stop," Susan said through rattling teeth. "That's the other part of the plan." She pointed up the hill. "Look, the pirates have their backs to the door, and the robots have surrounded them."

Aurora wasn't appeased. "Badger," was all she said. She scowled at Susan.

"Right." Susan pulled her sweatshirt down snuggly. She grabbed Taki's arm. "Ready?" she asked him.

Taki sighed. "I guess this is going to be Lesson Three, huh?"

Susan nodded.

"But," Aurora relaxed a little, "you don't know what it's like in the ship. How can you go there?"

Susan nodded and smiled at her. "Taki knows," she said.

Susan waved her arms around the clearing. "Maybe while we're gone, you could get some of the robots to clean up this mess. Maybe you should check whether any of our prisoners need first aid."

Susan turned to the line of boxes. "Wow," she added. "I never thought about whether the boxes had holes so they could breathe."

Aurora gasped. "I didn't either." She hurried off to check.

"We'll go get Badger," Susan called after her.

Aurora waved her arm as she hurried over to the line of boxes, calling for Sassy as she went.

Susan turned to Taki. "Ready?" she asked.

Taki shook his head, took a deep breath, and closed his eyes.

Susan pictured the garden by the shed.

They went.

46

Lesson 3

Taki stumbled as they landed by the water tap and the garden seat."I'm sure not used to that yet."

Susan put out a hand to steady him. "You do get used to it. You need to."

Taki took a deep breath. "OK, bring on Lesson Three."

Susan explained how she visualized the place she wanted to go.

"It's not just what you can see that is part of your image," she told him. "It's also the smells and sounds. Even the temperature helps get your image correct. So," she continued, "now I need you to visualize the place inside the ship that you know the best.

Where we won't be seen arriving. Get a whole picture of yourself there. And then tell your crystal that you want to be there."

"OK." A look of concentration came over Taki's face. He started to fade away.

Susan grabbed at him. "Hey, wait for me. I need to come with you so you can get back."

***

They landed on a floor in the dark.

Susan held onto Taki by a mere wisp of his sleeve. Susan wriggled around to sit up straight—and banged her head.

"Ow, where are we?"

"This is the cupboard they locked me in," Taki answered.

"We're locked in a cupboard! Why did you bring us here?"

"Take a deep breath."

Susan did and choked.

"This isn't a cupboard," she choked again, "it's a sewer."

She felt Taki's shoulder shrug against her arm. "Not exactly. There's a leak in the sewer pipe that runs through here on the way to being evacuated into space. When you said about smells being part of my image of a place, I knew I could get to here."

Susan tried not to take a breath. She patted Taki's arm and hoped she sounded encouraging. "Let's get out of here and find Badger as quickly as we can."

"OK."

They stood carefully. Susan's eyes had adjusted to the dark. A little light seeped in under the door. She saw Taki feeling for the door latch.

Click.

Click, click, click.

"It's locked." Taki slumped to the floor. "We're locked in. Just like I was." He shook his head. "How could I have been so stupid?"

"Hey, hey," Susan squatted in front of him, "that was your first use of your crystal. We're here. We didn't leave any parts of ourselves behind in the forest."

She slewed around and sat next to him again. "You've had the crystal for about three hours now," she told him. "You're doing great." She sighed. "But now you're going to have to do it again. We need to get moving, and we need to hurry."

Taki drew a large, calming breath and choked. "We have to get out of here." He gasped.

"Yep, we do. But we can't hop around all over the place. We're using up your energy doing this. So think. Where will Badger be?"

Taki went quiet. His body stilled. Susan grabbed hold of his arm again.

Susan felt the familiar blurring of the world around her, and when everything whirled back into focus, she and Taki stood in a large, open living area.

On instinct, they immediately turned back to back so that between them they could see the entire room. One end looked like a spaceship control center from a TV set. Monitors crowded the walls, and instruments covered the consoles.

Fancy chairs were placed so that the occupants could watch the monitors and instruments.

The rest of the room held tables, chairs, and what looked like a simple kitchen. Couches lined the walls. In one corner, a spiral staircase led both up to the deck above and down to the deck below.

"They call this area the mess," Taki whispered.

"Mess is right," Susan muttered. "Didn't anyone ever clean up in here?"

Taki shrugged. "That was my job. I didn't see why I should push myself for this lot."

"Huh." Susan elbowed him in the ribs. "Good point. No Badger though. Where's the next possibility?"

"I don't know." Taki looked around. "I thought this'd be where they'd throw him."

Susan thought a moment. "He was struggling pretty hard when they laid him on that log to haul him up to the ship. Maybe he's where they stowed the wood."

Taki nodded. "They would want to hurry back to haul in more, I guess."

"Well, let's go."

"Can't." Taki shook his head. "I've never been down there."

Susan clicked her tongue "Well, feet work too." She turned to him. "Do you think they left anyone on board? Should we be watching for stray pirates?"

“Captain Eames ordered everyone out to help. That’s why I was out there.” Taki laughed. “He thought the place was controlled by just the AI, and he’d been told it was compromised.”

Susan harrumphed as they moved toward the staircase. “Didn’t he get a surprise.”

Susan took the first step down. Taki grabbed her arm and pulled her back.

He held up his finger. “Look first, just in case,” he said. And with that, he sprawled on the floor and peeped over the edge so he could look down the stairwell. “All good,” he reported as he climbed to his feet again.

He brushed at his pants. Most of the crumbs and dust came away, but there was a goopy something stuck to his knee. Taki picked at it. The goop didn’t move. He sighed.

Susan laughed. “Come on. Down we go. You’re starting to look as scuffed up as the rest of us.”

Down they went. Both wore soft-soled shoes, so they made little noise on the steps. They passed one level. Corridors branched off from the landing. They saw nobody and heard no sounds over the steady background hum of the ship at rest.

Before they reached the next level down, Susan could smell the cut wood. The fresh pine scent drifted up the stairs to meet them. Susan felt the little hairs in her nose tickle as she relaxed and took deep breaths of something other than sewer.

“Don’t think I can’t hear you coming just because you’re trying to be quiet,” somebody yelled from below. “I’ve been smelling you for ages.”

"Badger?"

"Susan? How come you stink?"

Susan and Taki clattered down the final stairs to find themselves in the cargo hold of the Rum Punch.

Badger raised his head from where he lay strapped to a log. "Oh no, they captured you too?"

It took Susan a moment to catch up. "Uh, Badger this is Taki. Taki this is Badger." She waved her hand between the two. It felt silly to be making formal introductions at a time like this.

"Pleased to meet you." Taki put his hand out, as though to fist bump.

Badger tried to reach his hand out, but couldn't raise it far because of the strap binding his arms to his sides.

"Grrr, get me out of here. Explain later. They could return any minute." Badger wriggled and thrust against the binding straps.

"Stop that. It's not helping." Susan noticed chaffing on Badger's arms and legs. He'd obviously been desperately struggling against the straps. Susan turned to Taki. "Can we find something to cut the straps?"

Taki shook his head. "I don't think so. That's tetracarbon strapping. Not much will cut that."

Susan knelt down to peer underneath the log. "Well, there must be buckles or something. We need to free him so we can get out of here."

Taki climbed to the other side of the log and began searching there. "I've found it," he called.

Susan sighed. "Great. Undo it. Let's go."

Badger kept chanting. "Hurry, hurry, hurry."

Taki stood, frowning. “It’s locked with a computer code,” he said. “Only the computer can open the locks.”

“Let’s go.” Badger twitched on his log. “They’ll be here with more logs soon.”

Susan laughed a little. “I don’t think so. All the devices have them bailed up against the doors, which AI closed.”

This rescue was taking too long, though.

“Why don’t you just take us out of here?” Taki asked. “You’ve been jumping people around for ages. Let’s go.”

Susan looked down at Badger. The straps dug sharply into his body. One around his chest and arms, the next around his waist, and another just above his knees. She had a horrible vision of jumping them out of the cargo hold and finding Badger in pieces on the other side. Dead.

“Where’s the computer?” she asked. “Can we hack into it? Can we get Karst to hack into it?”

Bang. Somewhere on the ship, a door burst open. The sound of loud voices and yelling drifted down the stairwell.

“They’re back.” Taki gasped. “Hide.”

The two ducked down behind the log. Badger lay very still. They heard running feet overhead. “Batten down.” They heard the order.

Taki grabbed Susan’s arm. “They’re going to make a run for it. We have to go. You’ll have to risk it with Badger.”

Susan stood, uncertain. How could she take such a risk? All Badger and his family had wanted was freedom in a livable place where they could be useful and safe, and now, because of other people's greed, he was in such danger.

Susan looked at the length of the log. Could she take the whole thing? She sighed. She had to.

"Taki, hang onto my shoulder," she ordered.

Taking a deep breath, she placed one hand on Badger's chest. The other she placed on the log by his head. She pictured the clearing, every detail she could think of—the broken branches, the devices moving along the paths, Aurora and Sassy.

The cargo hold began to blur.

Wait. She thought of dropping in there with this huge log. What if it landed upside down? Badger would be crushed.

All the sounds were running together.

Or they could land on Aurora, and she would be crushed.

All the colors of the cargo bay were merging into one color: gray.

Wait. Where could they go?

Where would it be safe for them to land?

Arc Lake. They needed to land in water. Susan shut her eyes. She'd never changed her mind about her destination before.

"Come on, Crystal. You can do it. Into the lake we go."

47

Hold your breath

Splash!

Down Susan sank.

Her feet touched the mud, and she pushed up as hard as she could.

Air. Wonderful air. Susan took a deep breath and looked around. Yes, they were in the lake. She heard geese honking in alarm.

She felt the water surge behind her and, turning, saw one end of the log rear up out of the water. There was Badger still strapped tight. The log smacked down onto the surface. As Susan watched, the log rolled. Badger's weight pulled him under—under the water.

Susan swam over to the bobbing log. She dived down to Badger and tried to lift him up. Kicking as hard as she could, she managed to roll the log so that Badger was above water.

"Are you alright?" Susan gasped.

Badger nodded and swallowed. "Where's the other kid?"

Susan looked around. "Taki," she called.

No answer.

"Taaaaaakiiiiiii," she yelled.

No answer. "I think he was trying to tell you that he can't swim, right there before we jumped," Badger pointed out.

"Not at all?"

Badger shook his head. "Probably born in a dome. No swimming pools there. Water's pretty precious."

Susan looked around. She tried to peer over the top of the log.

"Can you see him?"

Badger shook his head.

"OK, I guess I'll have to look for him."

But if she let go of the log, Badger's weight would roll him over.

"Take a deep breath. I'll be as quick as I can."

"Oh, great." Badger took three quick breaths, then a very deep one. With his mouth puffed up, he nodded to Susan and shut his eyes. She let go of the straps, and the log rolled.

Susan dived quickly.

Their arrival in the lake had stirred up the mud. She couldn't see far into the roiling water. How could she find Taki in all this mess?

She realized she could use the murkiness. Wouldn't Taki be kicking and struggling? Susan peered around for the most swirling mud and swam over as quickly as she could.

Yes, a foot kicked out of the swirl. Then a hand. She grabbed for it and eased her way along until she felt his shoulder. Then she pushed him upward to the surface, kicking as hard as she could. She felt when he broke through into the air. His lungs gasped. She popped up next to him, with a smile.

Taki grabbed at her. She sank. He tried to climb on top of her.

She kicked off the bottom. This time she came up a little distant from him.

"Stop struggling," she yelled at him. "Roll onto your back," she ordered.

Taki choked. Spat up water. "I'm drowning."

"No you're not," Susan assured him. "Lie on your back." She told him.

"I'm drowning," Taki spluttered.

"No you're not. But Badger is. You have to come and help me save him."

"Oh." Taki carefully rolled onto his back. "Now what?"

"Take deep breaths and kick your legs," Susan ordered.

To avoid being pulled under again, Susan ran her fingers into his hair, and once she had a firm grip, she kicked out too, heading for the bobbing log.

As soon as they reached the log, Susan pulled Taki's hands onto one of the straps. "We have to roll it," she explained.

Taki nodded. They pulled together. The log rolled.

Badger rose to the surface. "Glad to see you." He spat up water.

Tears came to Susan's eyes. Only then did she understand how close to dying Badger had been. She dunked her head so that the tears weren't obvious to the boys.

Between Susan and Taki, they were able to push the log into shallow water near the shore. They wedged the log into the mud so it wouldn't roll over again. But they still hadn't solved the problem of getting Badger unstrapped.

What a wet and bedraggled trio they made.

Susan pulled at one of the straps, hoping that the water may have loosened them.

"Ow." The strap dug deeper into Badger's chest.

Taki twanged one of the bindings. "We're probably going to have to saw the log into bits to release him."

"That'll take ages." Susan sighed.

"Yeah, and I'm cold," Badger added.

Taki shook his head. "We need help."

Susan had an idea. She looked at Badger and saw that he had the same one.

"Karst," they said together and laughed.

Taki looked from one to the other. "Huh?"

Susan waved her hand at Badger. "He'll explain," she said. "I'm off."

Quickly, she formed a picture of the control room. And her crystal took her there.

48

Trust

She arrived along the back wall of the control room. Karst and Squirrel gazed intently at the monitor in front of them.

"Ahem." Susan wanted to let them know she had arrived.

Squirrel turned briefly. "Oh, hi," she said and turned back to the screen.

Susan squelched over to stand beside the other two. Her eyes followed theirs to the screen, which kept alternating between a wide view of the cargo bay and a view of the bay doors sliding open to reveal nothing. Blackness.

Susan peered and saw a few twinkling lights. The longer she looked the more she saw. *They're stars!*

Susan gasped. She was looking out into the vastness of outer space.

The view changed to show the cargo bay again. The Rum Punch lifted from the floor and drifted gently out through the doors. Once clear, the ship rocketed away.

"You let them get away?"

Squirrel and Karst sighed together. They'd been holding their breath.

"Oooh, you're all wet." Squirrel squeezed some water out of her sleeve.

"You let them get away?" Susan yelled.

Karst shrugged. "What would you suggest that we do?" He turned with his hands on his hips. "That captain threatened to use his cannons to blow the door open."

<We decided that this was the safest course of action.>

Karst nodded. "We worked it out, and it would require at least two Earth years to rebuild the cargo bay before it would be safe for another ship to arrive."

<This would have incapacitated our abilities to function.>

"Besides," Squirrel piped up, "AI slipped a coded beacon onto their ship. Their pirating days are numbered now."

<I detect excessive amounts of fluid on the floor of my control room. Analysis deems it to be H_2O with extraneous soil and a little algae also present.>

Susan shook her head. “Oh yes, we must hurry. We need your help, Karst. I came to get you.”

Karst backed up and shook his head. “I can’t leave AI.”

“Bring that little AI connector thingy you have and come. Badger needs you.” Susan pulled the two of them close.

“Ew, wet.”

“Badger never needs me,” Karst declared.

“Well, he does now,” Susan told him.

Susan pictured the scene by the pond—Badger on the log and Taki standing by, the water, the trees, the ducks, the geese.

They went.

***

As they faded into existence by the pond, Susan could see that the two boys were chatting.

“Well, there are actually six ponds equally balanced, so as not to upset the gravity spin,” Badger explained to Taki, who was looking all around.

Taki pointed up. “I still can’t get used to the sight of treetops and land and paths up there.” He shook his head in wonder.

The two noticed the trio as they became fully visible.

“About time,” Badger muttered. Susan noticed that his teeth were chattering.

Squirrel rushed to Badger. “What happened to you?” she wailed, looking all over the log and the strapping.

Susan pushed Karst forward. “Badger can explain what happened to him. It will take AI to undo the buckles. They’re coded.”

But Squirrel had noticed Taki. “Who are you?” she demanded.

“Um,” Taki reached across Badger and held out his hand, “my name is Taki.”

Squirrel thrust her hands behind her back and glared. “How did you get here? Who brought you?”

Karst came to stand beside her. “You must be from the pirate ship.”

Taki nodded slowly. “Um, yes, I was aboard the Rum Punch for a while, but . . .”

Karst didn’t wait for an explanation. He pulled out his AI connector. “We have another pirate prisoner here AI. Send a couple of fifty-sixes to throw him in with the others,” he ordered.

Badger chuckled. “My, listen to Mr. Bossy here,” he said. He reached his hand out and was just able to reach Karst’s shirt. He gave it a tug to get his attention. “Taki is one of the good guys, Karst.” He wriggled as much as the straps would allow. “Get AI working on getting these straps off me, please.”

Squirrel sniffed. “Well, if you say so. We’ll see.” She moved around the log to stand closer to Taki. “Explain yourself,” she ordered.

Susan butted in, “Not now, Squirrel. I want to take him with me. We need to bring back food and warm clothes. Aurora doesn't know that we rescued Badger yet."

"Rescued?" Squirrel turned all her attention to Badger. "Explain."

She sat crossed-legged on the log and took Badger's head into her lap. "I want to hear the whole story."

Karst bent down, and Susan could hear him quietly chatting with AI as he examined the first buckle.

Susan beckoned to Taki, and they moved a few paces away.

Karst looked up, attracted by their movement. "I got AI to let Sassy know that Badger was OK. They will meet you at the camp."

Susan nodded. Trust Karst to think ahead.

Taki and she joined hands, and Susan asked her crystal to take them to the campsite.

49

Back at Camp

Susan and Taki arrived a little on the pond side of Camp Bask. Susan stood on her tiptoes trying to find Aurora in among all the robots and devices hovering around the site.

"Wow, you kids are really organized." Taki looked over at the campsite. "Is that a Kitchentoto?" he asked pointing at the stove.

"I think that's what Aurora called it" Susan laughed. "She's over there." Susan indicated with her head where Aurora stood by the cubbies, ordering the smaller devices into tidy up mode.

Sassy nudged at Susan's leg. "We were worried about you," it announced. "Especially when the pirates broke through the tunnel access hatch."

Susan knelt and tried to give it a hug. It didn't work out well. Sassy had too many corners. "I've missed you," she told it. "We heard them coming," she started her story, "but it meant we had to leave in a hurry, and that's why we're down at the next pond."

"Um, I think I'll get started collecting blankets and clothes for Badger," Taki said and hurried off in Aurora's direction.

Susan nodded and continued her story. Sassy flipped up its lid, revealing one slice of pizza inside. "We had to feed the prisoners," it told her. "I tried to save you more, but they grabbed it before I could slam the lid."

"Hope you caught some of their fingers," Susan muttered, pulling a string of cheese into her mouth. The pizza was still warm and tasted so good.

"How many prisoners do we have?' she asked, munching happily.

"Six," Sassy answered. "They are not happy. Their captain abandoned them."

"What did they expect a pirate like him to do? I'm not surprised he left without them."

The two strolled up toward the camp. Well, Susan strolled; Sassy rolled.

Susan stopped. "Hey, I've just noticed that you're off the pathway. How do you manage that?"

Sassy laughed and whirled to show off its new mobility.

"AI decreed that I needed to be able to go where you go, so I went to the workshop and had larger outer wheels fitted to negotiate uneven terrain. They fold up for more speedy movement in the tunnels."

"Very nice." Susan smiled. She felt her shoulders let go as though the tension held there was releasing. Everything was turning out for the best. They were all safe, and the pirates were gone. New Hope was once again in its proper orbit. Taki was rescued. The blue crystal had a new Keeper.

I guess I'll be leaving soon. I should say goodbye.

She stepped up onto the flooring of the campsite.

"I won't be staying." Taki's chin stuck out, and his hands were on his hips.

"It's just a sleeping room." Aurora pointed to where two of the larger devices were pushing another cage into place.

"Yesterday, it was a cage."

"So?"

"I'm not sleeping in a cage."

"Would you rather be sleeping on the Rum Punch?"

Silence.

Susan chuckled to herself. Aurora won that round.

When Aurora turned to face her, Susan saw that she knew she'd won too. Taki just looked puzzled.

Susan rubbed her hands together. "Right," she said. "We need to get back to the others. Badger needs dry clothes and food." She pulled at her tunic. "We do too."

"Right." The tension eased. Aurora bustled around finding a change of clothes for Taki and Susan and more for Badger.

"I think you should take Aurora and the clothes and some food to the pond," Susan said to Taki.

"But . . ." Both Aurora and Taki spoke at once.

"Taki needs to practice crystalling," Susan informed them. "I don't think I'll be in New Hope much longer."

"What! Why?"

"Well, everything is fine now. The emergencies are all over, so that's my job done. I usually leave then. I just want some time to absorb this wonderful place before I'm gone."

Taki looked a little uncertain.

Susan made shooing motions. "You can do it. Go."

She watched the look of concentration grow on Taki's face. She saw Aurora grasp his hand. As they blurred and faded, both were smiling.

With that done, Susan looked around for Sassy.

"We'll take the paths, Sassy. I want to look around before I go."

"Very well, Susan," Sassy replied, and the two set out for Arc Lake.

50

Olympia Segunda?

By the time Sassy and Susan arrived, Karst and AI had managed to release the strap that bound Badger's chest.

"One off. Two to go," Badger informed them as they joined the group.

Karst muttered something. Squirrel interpreted. "Each strap has a different code," she explained. "We hoped that one code would handle all the buckles."

"At least I can breathe easier now." Badger waved his fingers.

Aurora held another piece of cheese to his mouth, and Badger opened wide. While he munched, Aurora told Susan of their plans.

"We're thinking of calling the log 'Badger's Folly.'" She waved her arms to show how they would position the log on the bank.

"We'll carve seats in it," Squirrel chipped in.

"I think we should push it out into the water and let it float around so that the birds have a safe place to sit where the land creatures can't get at them," Badger added his ideas to the mix.

Susan laughed. It was good to see the family all together and able to still share jokes and teasing. "I think Badger should carve his initials into it."

Aurora jumped up and came over to Susan. "No, Susan, you should carve your initials. You saved Badger. I can't imagine how you managed to bring this huge log out of the ship and all this way."

Badger started wriggling. "There's a knife in my pocket. Get started," he said. "Aurora thinks you might be leaving us soon."

Squirrel jumped up and hugged Susan's waist. "Don't go. We need you here. I've got so many questions to ask about your time."

Susan laughed and hugged her back. "It's not always my choice. Once everything is settled and the problem has been solved, usually my crystal pulls me back to my time. After all, I left in the middle of my birthday party back home."

Susan looked up. Everyone was staring at her.

"You mean if you're still here, there's more danger coming?"

"Um, usually." Susan watched the laughter fade from all the faces. "This is only my fourth adventure. I'm sure I still have a lot to learn."

She hurried to explain. "Maybe I've got that bit wrong. I haven't got the instruction sheet, so I'm learning as I go along."

"Waist strap done," Karst called.

Aurora reached over and pulled the strap free from Badger's waist. "You can sit up now," she told him.

Badger tried. He tried again. He groaned. Taki hurried over and grabbed one shoulder while Aurora grabbed the other. Together, they helped Badger to sit up. "Ow, sore muscles."

"You haven't moved for so long." Aurora pulled his tunic off over his head and began massaging his back muscles. With his arms free, Badger began moving them to get the feeling back.

Susan picked up one of the rugs they had brought. "Sassy, do you think you could make this warm? Not really hot, just warm?"

Sassy's top lid flew open. "That will take... twenty-three point eight seconds," it announced.

Susan stuffed in the rug and shut its lid.

Ding. *Sounds like a microwave,* Susan thought.

Sassy's lid flew open, and Susan pulled out the warm rug. She draped it over Badgers shoulders.

Badger sighed with relief. "I can feel the muscles loosening up."

Aurora smiled.

Susan picked up Badger's dry shirt and took it to Sassy. "Another twenty-three point eight seconds please, Sassy," she said.

Ding.

They pulled the warmed shirt over Badger's head.

"Third buckle open," Karst announced.

"At last." Badger swung his leg over and tried to jump to his feet. He collapsed into the mud beside the logs.

"Ow, fierce pins and needles." He groaned.

Taki and Aurora rushed in to start massaging the feeling back into his legs.

Squirrel helped Karst to stand. He'd been squatting for ages as he worked with AI to decode the buckles.

Susan had a quiet word on the side with Sassy, who bobbed once. Susan watched as its lights flashed gold, then green, then ran all around, flowing back and forth in patterns that were too quick for Susan to decipher.

"It will be here soon, Susan," it announced.

Badger was sitting on the log. Taki and Aurora pulled his arms over their shoulders and lifted him to his feet.

"You'll have to walk, Badger. It's getting dark. We need to get to the campsite."

Susan looked up in surprise. Yes, she hadn't noticed the light dimming around them. Soon it would be totally dark. No moon or streetlights here.

She heard the whir of wheels on the path.

She turned with a smile toward the others. "Badger, I think your chariot awaits." She made a grand gesture with her arm and timed it perfectly as one of the larger devices came rolling towards them. A chair from the campsite stood on top of the box, and the device's arm held it in place. The device spun in place so it was facing back toward home.

Badger hooted. "Just for me." With Taki and Aurora to help, he hobbled over.

The device lowered its arm, and Badger was able to step into it. Up he went and sat carefully in the chair. The device shone a light ahead, and the others all gathered around as they set off toward the campsite.

It's starting to feel like a home, Susan realized.

It was completely dark now, and they followed the beam of light. Sounds of night creatures filled the air. The buzz of insects. An owl hooting somewhere. There were scratchings and skitterings in the grass beside the path.

Taki moved closer to Susan. "What are all those noises?" he whispered.

"That's just the night creatures coming out to feed and to hunt," Susan assured him.

"In Olympia Segunda, the only noises we hear like that are the rodents in the walls and the cats that are chasing them," Taki told her.

"These are the normal night noises of a forest. You'll get used to it and will soon love it like I do." Susan patted his arm.

"That's why we built this, you know. So that people could have these experiences again, without having to go down to Earth. Most people can't afford to go down there to the nice places. We wanted New Hope to be the very best of what the Earth had been."

Susan tried to see his face clearly in the dark. "You built it?" she asked.

Taki fluttered his arm. "Um, I meant why it was built." He hurried forward and began talking to Aurora.

"Hmmmmm." Susan looked ahead. Camp Bask—home—came into view.

Susan stretched and yawned. She scratched her ribs. What a day.

The only thing I meant to do today was visit Titan. That's about the only thing I didn't do.

"Good night, Sassy. Good night, everyone." Susan crawled into her sleep cubby, and even after the excitement of the day, she fell asleep in moments.

51

Who is Taki?

When Susan opened her eyes, she could see light through the curtain of her cubby. She snuggled under the covers. *Today, I will definitely visit Titan*, she decided. *But not yet.* She took a deep breath.

Somebody tiptoed past her curtain. She couldn't tell who from the shadow they cast. *Maybe it was Taki. Six humans here now when it should just be creatures, plants and robots.*

Susan sat up with a groan. *I'm still here. What else can go wrong?*

She threw back her covers and crawled over her bed to peep out through the curtain. It was full daylight outside. Time to get up.

While Susan figured out how to work the shower, she washed her own clothes as well as she could. The warm water felt wonderful, sluicing off all the dust, mud, and other stuff that had accumulated. She scurried back into the clothes that Aurora had lent her and wrung as much water out of her jeans and sweatshirt as she could. *I guess I'll have to throw them over a bush to dry.*

Susan ran her fingers through her hair to set it in place. Once again, she was pleased it was so short. She sighed for the brush and comb she had in her 'go bag' at home.

"Good morning."

Susan turned quickly. Taki sat at the table in the eating area. He smiled and gestured at one of the seats. "There's only four seats, so better grab one quickly."Susan showed her wet clothes and nodded to the stove contraption. "I don't suppose that thing has a dryer in it somewhere?"

Taki smiled and shook his head. "Not that I can remember from the specs I read on this model."

"Oh well," Susan shrugged, "I guess it's the bushes then."

She stepped off the flooring and looked around for a suitable spot to spread her clothing.

Taki followed her. "I think everyone else is still sleeping."

With her clothing spread, the two of them wandered down to the pond and settled on the shoreline.

The two sat together, enjoying the atmosphere around them. The noise of birds, the rustle of trees, and all those sounds of nature amplified their comfortable silence. To Susan, it felt good to just sit and soak in the surroundings. As long as she didn't look up and ignored the way the horizon curved upward, she could believe she was close to her house. *Only about two hundred years and millions of kilometers away.* She sighed.

A skein of geese honked into view and skidded into the water. Taki drew back and frowned. "Is it safe to be here?" he asked.

"You don't know much about animals, do you?"

Taki grimaced. "We have cats to keep down the mice and rats in the dome. We had birds to start with, but their feathers drifted into the oxygen filters and clogged up the works. You can't have the oxygen filters malfunctioning, so the birds had to go."

Taki waved his hand at the scenery around them. "That's why we had to build this out here. The adults who were born on Earth could see that my generation was missing the experience of such a place. New Hope, we call it."

Susan scooched around so she could see Taki's face properly. "That's the second time you've said you had something to do with building this place."

"My dad and mum did," Taki confessed. "They're investors."

"Your family must be very rich."

Taki shrugged. “I suppose. My ancestor, Socrates, was a ship builder on Earth, in Greece. When the economy got rocky, nobody wanted ships any more. He had all these workers and their families, and he felt responsible. So, when the Great Exit began, he started building rockets and ships for space.

“On Mars, there’s a mountain called Olympia Mons, and that attracted his attention. It took a lot of effort and all his money. Some people died, but he built a dome on Mars for all our people who wanted to move. He called it ‘Olympia Segunda.’ I’m named after him, but I’ve shortened it to Taki.

“It was hard at first, but now we’re well established and comfortable in our dome. We use gravity boots and the floors in most of the dome are magnetized to help our bodies build. But we still need to experience full gravity.

“So, my mum and dad got some investors together when we held the first Mars Olympic Games . They all agreed to build New Hope. Our dome built the four leviathans.”

Susan didn’t know what to say. Taki’s story sounded like science fiction to her. She grabbed onto the one word that stood out to her.

“Games? You mentioned games. What games?”

Taki laughed. “I guess it does sound funny, but Grandfather wanted to continue the Greek tradition of the Olympic Games, so he started them up again with a Mars version.”

Susan laughed too and shook her head. “I can’t even imagine what sports you have with the low gravity.”

Taki grinned. "Yes, well, hammer throw is out. The jumping and foot races are pretty spectacular though. Gymnastics has gone three dimensional, and we've added trapeze. Water sports are out. We can't keep the water in the pool." Taki shrugged. "Wrestling and boxing work really well. I compete in the diving."

"I thought you said there were no pools."

Taki nodded. "Oh, it's different. We dive off a board, but we land on a net."

They sat in silence for a while. , Susan worked to get her head around sports played in low gravity.

Eventually Taki broke the silence. "We were on our way here in our space yacht when we were attacked by the Rum Punch."

"But, why were you coming here? From what the cousins told me, there isn't supposed to be anyone arriving for another year or two. There's no accommodation built."

Taki drew in a deep breath. He glared across the water. "And yet they're here. And this Alvion person you told me about. He came because something was wrong. My dad was investigating too. He'd been looking at the expenses and the progress of the site. We came to check it out. Dad was right. There's a lot wrong here. There's children. There's sabotage. There's destruction. And somewhere there's a rogue robot called Titan that has achieved sentience." He waved his arms at her. "It's all going to be fixed," he declared and stalked off up the beach.

Susan jumped up and ran after him. She grabbed his arm and turned him to face her. "New Hope would be in the Sun by now if it wasn't for the children. They returned us to our correct orbit, with the help of Titan—the rogue robot, as you call him. Karst was able to undo the override program placed in AI by the people you hired to create this place. The children are refugees. They're here so that they won't have to do some sort of debt thing on Earth. They called it inden . . . indent . . ." Susan waved her hand. "Something like that."

Taki nodded. "The word is indenture. In the domes, we consider it a form of slavery."

Susan shuddered. "How? . . . How could such a thing happen?"

Taki sighed and looked off into the distance. "There are always some people who think they should have power over others. It gets lots of names, but this debt thing that has sprung up on Earth is hard to fight. People need to eat and have a roof over their heads." Then he shook his head and straightened his tunic. "Anyway, they can't stay here. It's not theirs."

Susan frowned at him. "The children defended the forest from the pirates. To me, they are excellent custodians of New Hope. If everything is centered on money and debt now, maybe they should send you a bill for saving the place and routing the pirates before the forest was cleared. And, by the way, you've been rescued from the pirates too. I want them to be free." Susan tugged at her tunic for emphasis.

Taki let out a great huff of air. "Not everyone can be free."

Susan felt like kicking him. "Why not? Did you like being 'not free' in the pirate ship?"

Taki opened his mouth to speak, but Susan kept on. "We rescued you, and now you're free. Well, I want them to be free too. You're the Keeper of the Crystal for out here, in the Outer Regions. I think you need to have a good look at what that means. They don't even have parents to look after them out here."

Taki deflated on the spot.

Susan saw the change in him. His face crumpled and his body seemed to grow smaller and hunched in front of her. Why? Then she understood. Taki's father was dead and his mother missing. Why did she have to talk about parents? She reached out and gave Taki a hug. "I know you must be worried sick about your mother," she told him.

She felt his nod against her shoulder.

Susan pushed back to see his face. "We'll get Karst to ask AI to send out a message to all the proper people, and you'll be picked up." Susan shook his shoulders gently. "But I'd think very seriously before shipping the children away. They know how to live in this environment, and they will look after it and all the creatures. Their parents were the creators, you know."

Taki looked around. "They created this?"

Susan nodded. "Aurora told me that their family is indentured to the Sutton family, and they were contracted to do this work. They look after the Sutton Range Estates on Earth. Their parents sneaked them up here with the last shipment of animals so that they wouldn't be forced into debt on Earth. They sent them here, so they could live free."

Taki gave a wry smile. "Nothing's ever simple, is it?"

The two held hands as they walked back to camp.

52

We Want to Stay

The four cousins were clustered around the table when Taki and Susan arrived. Looking up, Aurora handed them each a round of flat bread. "I made some naan this morning," she told them.

Squirrel jumped up and moved to the stove. "I caught two more of the chickens." She returned to the table and spooned scrambled eggs onto their naan.

"Thanks." The smell of thyme mixed in the egg made Susan's tummy rumble. She carefully rolled the naan around the egg. It tasted great.

Badger jumped up. "Here, take my chair. Mum and Dad weren't planning on us having guests. We only have four chairs at the moment."

"Thanks." Susan slumped onto the offered chair.

Taki sat in the chair that Karst dusted off for him.

An awkward silence fell around the group. Susan and Taki ate in silence. Susan noticed the cousins exchanging glances among themselves.

Aurora eventually spoke. "I haven't found the pepper and salt yet, sorry."

Susan looked up sharply. She smiled. "Well, we have been quite busy since you got here. I think we can pass on the salt shakers."Taki swallowed the last of his egg wrap. "It's amazing to me that you can produce food at all in this place."

Badger stood abruptly from where he had been leaning on the bench. "OK, enough of this chit chat. What do we do now? We thought we would have a couple of undisturbed years here while the biosphere settled." He waved his arm at the surrounding forest. "Plenty of time to have made ourselves indispensable."

Aurora took up the story. "But now, there's Taki, and he'll need rescuing, and Titan sent out an alert to the owners, and we don't want to go back to Earth. We think New Hope needs us here. We want to stay."

"We want our parents to be here too," Squirrel said in a small shy voice. Karst grabbed her hand and nodded.

Everyone looked at Taki. He fiddled with a glass on the table. "I don't know what to say. I need to find out about my mum. I hope she's alright. I need to let my family know that I'm alive and well, and . . . and . . . that my dad is dead."

Aurora jumped up and moved around the table. She pulled Taki to his feet and enveloped him in a huge hug. "Oh, sorry. I forgot about that."

Squirrel joined the hug, pulling Karst with her. Badger looked at Susan, shrugged with a wry smile and joined the hug. Susan joined in too.

And that's when Karst's pocket started buzzing.

53

Incoming!

The six disengaged with a sigh.

Karst hauled out his communicator.

<Incoming. Incoming.> AI's loud announcement echoed through the forest.

Ducks flew off the pond in alarm. An eagle took to the air screeching. Squirrel stuck her fingers in her ears.

"We can hear you," Badger and Aurora yelled at the same time.

<Incoming. Incoming,> AI continued.

Karst held the communicator as far away from his ear as he could.

"What do you mean 'incoming'?" he asked.

<I've learned that that is the correct wording for announcing an arrival in the cargo bay. Titan allowed me access to his human television collection.>

Badger and Aurora stiffened and looked around, alarmed.

"Who is it this time?" Karst asked.

<It's a ship out of Glory Be named 'New Hope 2.' Registration GB38.>

Taki took two steps back. Susan noticed that his face looked frozen.

"AI, who is piloting?" Taki's words were casual, but Susan heard tension in every one.

<Piloted by Sirrah Veronica Brighton. They are requesting boarding. They have the topmost priority codes.>

Badger pulled at the hem of his tunic.

"Stall them, AI. Pretend there's a malfunction or something. Give us time."

Squirrel rushed toward her cubby. "I have a go bag ready," she yelled over her shoulder. "I will be ready to hide in no time."

Aurora turned to Karst. "Get your bag, Karst. It looks as though we will have to hide."

Susan looked around. "You can't hide all this." She knocked on the stove with her knuckles. "You are established here."

Aurora and Badger exchanged glances.

They look so scared, Susan noticed.

Badger sighed. “I’ll get the food stores and move them into the forest,” he said. “Maybe if we move as far aft as possible, they won’t notice us.”

“Maybe we could ask AI to confine them to the tunnels,” Aurora suggested hopefully as she gathered the plates and cups from the table.

Taki reached forward and shut the lid of the box Aurora was stacking the plates into. “Wait,” he said. “You can’t hide. They have sensors on their ship. And once they’re inside, they will monitor the entire place from the control room.”

Badger stepped right up into Taki’s face. “I suppose you think we should just walk right up there and greet them.”

Taki stepped back, but he nodded.

“Would you like us to hold our hands out in front so they can clap us in irons before they send us back to Earth and charge us for the trip?” Badger asked, with a sarcastic turn to his lip.

“I don’t think that will happen.”

Badger clenched his fists and moved a step closer to Taki. “Who are you?” he snarled. “Arrived on a pirate ship. Fancy clothes. Help us?” He stuck out his chin. “Maybe.”

“Please trust me on this.” Taki looked over to where Susan and Aurora stood watching. “I think you can convince them that you should remain.” Taki shook his head. “You can’t hide. Where are you going to go?”

Aurora moved over to stand beside Badger. She enclosed his fist in her hands. “He’s right,” she said.

"It was a nice dream and we have had a wonderful adventure, but we have no power here."

Susan moved up to join the group. "It's worth a try. Maybe you can convince them that it is safer to have you here. After all, you saved New Hope from destruction."

Aurora looked up with a spark in her eyes again. "That's right we did—well, with Titan's help. But we saved the trees."

"And you rescued me," Taki added.

"Hmph." Badger huffed. "It's not certain that's going to be in our favor. You came with the pirates."

Taki huffed in turn. "I was held for ransom."

"Yeah, yeah," Badger turned to Karst, "put your go bag back in your cubby. Ask AI to allow the ship in."

Karst looked at him, surprised.

Badger gave a sideways grin. "We're going to greet our visitors," he told him. "I just hope we don't get arrested," Badger muttered as he turned away.

Quickly the children sorted themselves out. Taki suggested that the four cousins and Susan should form the welcoming committee.

"Put on your best clothes and your bravest smiles," he recommended. "That's what my dad always said before a big meeting."

Susan saw Taki's face change. It crumpled as she watched. Taki slumped onto a chair and covered his face with his hands. Quiet sobs sneaked out between his fingers.

"Your dad." Aurora hurried over and put her arms around his shoulders.

She looked over at Badger with an inquiring look. Badger nodded once. "You can stay here with us, you know," Aurora added.

"We'll find another chair," Squirrel offered.

Taki rubbed his hand down his face. "That's generous of you. Thank you." He swallowed hard. "But I will have responsibilities at home. I will have to leave on New Hope 2." Taki drew a deep sobbing breath and mopped his face on his sleeve.

Aurora sent Squirrel and Karst to their cubbies to change into their best clothes. "Nothing with patches," she whispered.

Aurora pulled at Susan's sleeve. "You need something better to wear too." She motioned with her head toward her cubby.

Susan tiptoed after her. *Taki needs some time to himself.*

At her cubby, Aurora fished around in a box set into the corner. "Dad packed some of the clothes I'd grown out of. We figured Squirrel could use them." She held up a tunic made of an apple green material. It rippled through her fingers as she held it out to Susan. "I don't have any pants that will fit you though."

Susan poked at the tunic. "What's it made of?" It felt cool and so soft to her fingers. "It's beautiful." She sighed. "Thank you."

Aurora pulled it over Susan's head and patted it down into place. "It's bamboo," she said. "Most of our clothes are made of hemp." She plucked at her shirt. "Hemp isn't as soft." Aurora smoothed the fabric over Susan's shoulders.

"This was a gift from a resort guest," she explained. "We could never have bought something this fine."

The tunic reached almost to Susan's knees. "It feels lovely against my skin," she said.

Aurora nodded and turned back to find something that she could wear.

Susan used the time to straighten out the cover on the bed. She recognized the hummingbird duvet.

The two girls stepped out of the cubby, Susan in apple green and Aurora wearing a similar tunic in a deep rose red. They joined the others, who were standing in a row. *Almost at attention*, Susan thought as she and Aurora slipped onto the end of the line.

Taki was ordering the show. His back was straight; his gaze was steady. But Susan noticed that his eyes were red rimmed with held back tears.

"Now, you need to get down to the staging area." Taki walked along the line. "Don't enter the cargo bay. Just open the doors, so they will be drawn out into the biosphere. They will all be curious to see it. Invite them back here for tea. I noticed you have some here. Tea is scarce in the domes and out on the stations. They'll come for the tea."

Badger frowned. "And what are you going to be doing while we're off meeting who knows who?" he asked Taki

Taki waved his arm vaguely. "Oh, I'll have this place all ready by the time you return." He looked around the camp. "It needs a bit of a tidy up."

Susan clasped hands with the cousins. She pictured the ledge outside the cargo bay doors.

The camp around them blurred, and just as everything was going dim, she heard Taki.

“Good luck,” he called.

I hope I’m doing the right thing, trusting him.

The five arrived on the ledge.

54

Veronica, Marvin, and Raj

Sassy whirred up to stand beside Susan. "Did you know a ship is arriving?" it asked.

Susan knelt down beside Sassy. "Yes, we know. That's why we're here. What have you been doing?"

Sassy waved its arm at the clearing below them. "We started to clean up the pirates' mess," it declared.

Susan looked down into the forest. Most of the branches were trimmed from the logs. The others joined her on the edge. As they watched, one of robots thrust a branch into a hatch on its companion. There was a harsh buzzing noise, and it pulled out a trimmed stick, which it moved to a pile in one corner.

"AI thought we could make an interesting fence around the gravesite. It has Partition researching how that's done."

Aurora put her hands on Sassy's lid. "Please thank AI. That's a lovely idea."

<Ahem, I can hear you.>

"Um," Karst fumbled with his communicator, "AI, has the ship docked?"

<Equalizing atmosphere in the cargo bay. It will be normalized in two minutes, forty-five seconds.>

"AI, how many people onboard?"

<New Hope 2 informs me there are four humans, twelve robots—peacekeeper class—fourteen maintenance devices, and itself.>

The children looked at each other.

"Four humans." Squirrel danced a step. "I wonder who they are."

"I hope they're nice," Karst muttered.

"It's the peacekeeper robots I'm worried about." Badger growled.

"Let's be ready." Aurora set everyone in a line to the side of the door. "Remember to smile," she added, taking a deep breath.

"Wait." Susan looked at Karst. "We want them to come out this way, not through the tunnels to any Control Room."

<I heard that, Crystal Keeper. I will open the cargo bay door as soon as they disembark.>

Sassy turned to wheel back to the clearing.

Susan rapped its lid. "Stay with us, Sassy. Show your friendliest colors."

Sassy nudged into the line beside Squirrel and set its lights to a gentle blue, green, and white pattern.

They waited.

All the devices working around the fallen trees stopped work and aligned themselves in tidy rows. All faced toward the cargo bay.

"Sassy, did you organize that?" Susan asked in a whisper.

Sassy bobbed in place and spun its red lights once. "AI thought it might be a nice gesture."

They waited.

Slowly, the bay door slid open.

All the children took a deep breath. Aurora and Squirrel clasped hands.

They heard them before they saw them, two people arguing.

A man said loudly, "This has truly been a waste of time. There's nothing wrong here. Every instrument we checked came up optimal."

A woman replied angrily, "You didn't receive the distress signal. I did. You weren't invited along. You decided to come. You pushed your way onto our craft. There *was* something wrong when we first checked the orbit although now everything is working to expectations."

The same man said, still loudly, "I'm the contract manager. I had a right to be on your ship."

The voices were getting closer as the arguers moved closer to the door.

The children braced themselves.

Two people, a man and a woman, strode out onto the ledge. Their steps faltered as they took in the scene before them.

The woman gasped. “It’s magnificent! More than I could have ever imagined.” She moved to the edge and looked up. “There’s so much. Look, the tops of trees, instead of sky.” She staggered a step and clasped the shoulder of the man who joined her. “It’s a little disorienting.” She chuckled.

“So is that,” the man answered, pointing down into the clearing below.

The woman’s eyes followed his pointing finger. She gasped when she saw the fallen trees and the devices drawn up in ranks. “Oh dear, is it supposed to be like that, Marvin?”

Marvin didn’t answer because at that moment a third visitor strolled out through the door.

“I say,” the newcomer said, “my readings are showing unusual evidence.” He peered at an electronic device, which he held in one hand. As they watched, he shook his device and held it up to his ears. “Maybe it’s an anomaly of the asteroid.” He stroked the little screen again. “Nope, it’s still saying there are twelve other humans here besides us.” He jabbed the screen again. “And,” he added, “there’s an extra digital intelligence here.”

The newcomer joined the other two. Finally, he looked up from his device. “Amazing.” He breathed. “Splendid.”

"Not so, Raj." Marvin smirked. "Look beyond the screen in your hand, for once, and see what's happened at your feet."

Susan felt the tension rising in the cousins as they stood waiting to be noticed.

Badger took matters into his own hands. He shuffled his feet and cleared his throat. "Welcome to New Hope, Sirrahs," he announced loudly.

With a collective gasp, the newcomers twisted around to face the children.

Squirrel lifted her hand in a shy wave. The others stood unmoving.

The woman held a laser-like weapon in her hand. It pointed straight at them and never wavered. "I am Sirrah Veronica Brighton, appointed security watch for New Hope. Explain yourselves. Right. Now."

Marvin stepped behind her and peeped at the children over her shoulder.

Raj stepped up to the woman and pushed her weapon down. "Now, now, Veronica. These are children. Five children."

The woman shook off his hand. "They don't belong here. They're trespassing on our property. They've damaged our forest. Look at those cut trees. There was to be no logging for at least five more years. What will our tourists think when they come and that's the first thing they see?" Her weapon never wavered. But now it pointed directly at Badger. "Explain yourselves," she snarled.

Raj, who stood tall and straight, a man with a dark flowing beard, dressed in loose fitting white clothing and wearing a turban of the brightest blue, pushed her hand down again. "Listen to what I say, please, Veronica. There are *twelve* humans on this asteroid. Not to mention an unexplained intelligence. Five stand before us." He turned Veronica around so that she was looking out over the forest. "Now, where are those other seven? And what are they doing right now? We're a little exposed on this ledge, don't you think?"

Marvin whimpered and moved back from the edge.

Veronica huffed and slipped her weapon back into its holster.

Susan took that opportunity to step forward. "We welcome you," she announced. "We are the ones who sent the distress signal."

Badger took up the story. "But then we were able to fix the problem ourselves."

"With the help of Titan," Susan added. "We came up here to invite you to our camp where we have tea waiting."

"Your camp!" the woman yelled. "You're interlopers here. How dare you have a camp."

Susan moved a step closer. "Please join us. All will be explained."

The visitors looked doubtful.

"There is no danger to you here, I assure you." Susan gave her best smile and indicated the path down to the clearing below. "This is a place of true wonder," she added.

Marvin spoke up. "We don't need explanations. We should just take them and go. We can ship them back to wherever they came from when we're far away from here."

Veronica glared, but said nothing.

Raj grinned at the children. "Well, I, for one, want to hear what they have to say. A lot has been happening here that we know nothing about, and I need to understand. I'm official recorder for this facility. I want to know." He waved at the path. "Lead on," he told Susan.

And so Susan started off down the path. "Please, follow me."

55

Tea is Served

The group moved along the path, mostly in silence. Sirrah Veronica tut-tutted at the disarray still evident in the garden as they passed by. In fact, she took pictures of almost everything as they walked along the pathway.

When they reached the clearing holding the two graves, the visitors stopped short.

"And I suppose this is just for effect," Marvin sneered, nudging at the cross on Spruce's grave.

Karst kicked him in the shins. "That's our mum's grave, you . . ."

Aurora stood over Marvin where he rolled on the ground clutching his shin.

"Assault, assault! Arrest them all." Marvin groaned. "I'll have a bump. A bump."

Veronica hauled him to his feet. "Quit your whining," she told him and pushed him back onto the path.

Susan noticed Raj beside the other grave. He had fallen to his knees. She went over to him.

"Did you know Alvion True?" she asked.

Raj nodded. "We've been looking for him. He disappeared from his office. He works with computers and artificial intelligence, you know, and sometimes he would shut himself in his office for days, so nobody was too worried, until he missed his mother's birthday. Nobody saw him leave. We had no idea where he went." He reached forward and gently stroked the ID tag that hung on the stick marking the grave. "How did he get here? How did he die?"

Susan sighed and sank down to sit beside Raj. "Your first question, I will show you later." She marked it off on her fingers. "Your second question is part of the explanation of what's been happening here."

Raj sat back and stared at her. "And I suppose I will only have your word for it."

Susan glared at him. "You should be thanking us not accusing us. Alvion left a recording. He was murdered."

Raj looked down his nose at her. "Well, a recording, *you* say. I'll believe it when I see it. You are the ones who are breaking the law here."

Susan reached forward and straightened the ID tag on the post.

"It's hard for me to see this situation from your perspective. I've been living it, and it's still hard for me to believe all that's happened." She climbed to her feet. "It's not much further to camp now. We'll tell you all we know."

Susan looked around. The others had moved off along the path. They were still arguing. She held her hand out to Raj. "Come on. We should catch up before they arrive."

Raj groaned to his feet. "Too long on a spacecraft is not good for my fitness levels."

"Oh, you can get plenty of exercise here," Susan assured him. "If we don't catch up, you'll be breaking up a fight."

"Hmm, yes, that Badger is a little short tempered."

Susan nudged his arm. "I was thinking about Sirrah Veronica."

Raj gave a short laugh. "Yes, OK, her too."

The two jogged to catch up with the others.

***

The group entered the encampment together.

Everything was tidy. Every cubby curtain was closed. All the extra dishes and cooking utensils were stowed—somewhere. The table had a cloth over it. (Susan recognized the sheet from her bed.) Cups and mugs were laid out on the table, as were spoons.

Sugar was set out in a small bowl, and water was boiling on the Kitchentoto.

Susan cast her eye around. Taki was nowhere to be seen. She noticed Aurora looking too. Their eyes met, and they shrugged. Meanwhile, Badger was politely conducting the three adults to the table and seating them in the chairs. Aurora hurried to the stove to make the tea, and Squirrel plumped herself down on a box that was padded with a pillow. She immediately started peppering Marvin with questions.

Karst just stood. Susan pushed him gently to another box so that he, too, could sit at the table.

Aurora brought the steaming pot over. "We don't have any cookies to offer you. I'm sorry," she said. "I haven't had time for baking lately."

"You could bake here? On that thing?" Marvin waved his hand toward the Kitchentoto.

Raj leaned forward and nudged him hard. "That's the latest model."

Veronica turned to Badger. "How have you acquired such an item?" She wanted to know.

Badger glared at her. "It is the one our parents sent with us. They are in debt for a further two years for it." He locked eyes with Veronica. "Not that they'll ever get out of debt even though they work hard all the time."

Veronica looked a little uncomfortable under Badger's stern glare. She fiddled with the badges pinned to her chest. "Yes, well, we know it's hard for people on Earth, b—"

"Hard." Badger's voice rose in volume. "Hard. You know nothing and care nothing."

Aurora stood. "I'll pour the tea, shall I?" She met Badger's eyes and signaled him to shut up. "It's important that we tell you what happened here. New Hope could still be in danger." She carefully poured the tea into the waiting cups and mugs.

A wonderful aroma of green tea with jasmine wafted over the table. Everyone paused to breathe deeply. The mood of the group calmed.

Raj raised his mug. "There is peace to be had in sharing together." He smiled.

Veronica huffed. "Yes, well, I need an explanation. There's a lot wrong here, and I need to get to the bottom of it."

"Ahem." Taki stepped out of his cubby and rose to stand tall. He walked over to join them.

Marvin leaped to his feet. "Sirrah Socrates, you are found." He rushed over to hug the boy. Susan saw Taki flinch back from the rush. He gave her a wink over Marvin's shoulder.

Raj rose as well. He walked over and gently pulled Marvin away from his prolonged hug. Raj held out his hand. "It is so good to see you safe," he said. The two shook hands.

"You knew I was missing?"

"Yes, yes." Marvin waved his hand. "We intercepted your craft on our way here." He moved in for another hug. "It's wonderful. We've rescued you too." He beamed around at everyone. "We'll be famous." He threw his arm around Taki's shoulders.

Taki shrugged away and turned his attention to Raj. "My m . . ." He got no further.

Raj grinned broadly. "She's on our ship, son. She's in the infirmary. Why don't you go and say hello. She's been very worried about you."

Taki took off, running down the path.

Raj turned his attention to his communicator. "I'll just let our AI know he's coming." He turned to the children. "This is wonderful. Everyone has been so worried about him."

Sirrah Veronica wriggled in her seat. "His mother said he'd been taken by pirates." She glared at the children.

With a happy sigh, Marvin sat back at the table. "Doesn't matter now. He's found. We'll be famous. There's probably a reward. We rescued him."

Badger leaned across the table. "No. We rescued him. We saved him from the pirates. We have six captives. They'll be pirating no more."

Raj leaned back in his chair. "There is obviously a long story to tell here. I think we should get started."

Veronica straightened her back and spread her hands on the table. "I'll hear it." She scowled. "But I'll be checking the facts."

56

The Story is Told

Susan let the cousins tell the story. She sat back and watched the reaction of the listeners. All three were cross and frowning when the children told the story of how they came to be on New Hope. All looked in awe at the forest, ponds all around and over them, when the children explained the part their parents had played in creating the biosphere of the asteroid.

Then it was Susan's turn to explain about Alvion True. Marvin looked uncomfortable.

Veronica made furious notes on her electronics. Raj reminded her that he wanted to see the recording.

When she told of the three men who delivered the last load of animals, and of the one who tampered with the AI, Marvin blustered about the stupidity of the story. But when Susan described the holomessage she had watched, where the Suttons gave their final instructions, Marvin went very, very quiet. Susan saw his face pale. He was sweating. He looked around, as if something was about to spring out of the woods and kill him on the spot.

"You have a recording of that message, right?" Veronica demanded. Slowly Susan shook her head. "Sassy, didn't record it. I didn't think to ask it to. Sorry."

Veronica sniffed in disapproval. "No proof. Just your word." She looked Susan up and down. "There's not been any explanation about who you are and where you're from."

Raj tapped the table with his fingers. "Let's get on with the main story, shall we?" He looked around the table. "There's a lot more to tell."

The children nodded. And the story continued.

Between them, Badger and Squirrel recounted the story about finding Titan and the way he had stopped the rockets firing and returned them to orbit. Squirrel went off into explaining what a wonderful place Titan had created for himself and how clever he was.

Raj looked extremely interested. "He had an avatar, you say?"

Badger nodded. "He made that geode beautiful inside."

Susan watched Raj, Marvin, and Veronica exchange significant looks between them.

They seemed a little too interested in Titan. "Tell about how Karst undid the programming," she prompted.

And so the story went on.

The pirates arrived and started cutting down trees. They rescued Taki. They organized the devices to defend the trees.

Susan saw Badger open his mouth to explain how she and Taki rescued him from the pirate ship, but she gave her head a quick shake. Badger saw it and clamped his mouth shut.

"'erm 'erm." He picked up the story. "We captured six of the pirates. AI has them locked up somewhere."

There was silence around the table.

Aurora let out a heavy sigh. She stood. "I'll make more tea, shall I?" she said and moved over to the Kitchentoto.

Marvin wriggled in his seat. "Load of nonsense." He ran his finger around his collar as though he was choking. "Bunch of children left on their own, probably sat around. Made the whole thing up." Nobody interrupted his rant, so he continued. "Accusing the Suttons of such goings on. Why, they've been behind this project from the start. Supplied the expertise." He waved at the cousins. "OK, so that was their parents—but they work for the Suttons. The animals are from their reserves." He looked round at the forest and the pond. "They're out there, just as the contract states." He thumped the table for emphasis. "I have the pictures they sent. They delivered everything as promised." He opened the collar of his jacket. "They didn't deliver children."

He looked at Veronica and Raj. "Can't you tell when you're being fed a pack of lies?"

Veronica looked up from her electronics. "Our AI has pin-pointed the location of the six prisoners. It will be interesting to hear what they have to say. I'm sending the peacekeepers to pick them up and take them to our ship."

Raj took up the conversation. It was as if the children were not even there. Just children. Adults talking over their heads. "I'm most interested in this Titan. It could be a big advance for us. From what they say, it has achieved a big step forward in AI ability to reason and think. We need to get him downloaded and back into a laboratory, so we can run tests. It could be dangerous."

Marvin nodded eagerly. "Yes, that geode sounds interesting too. It's made a great place there. Imagine how much we will be able to charge for people to visit. Or, or we could make it accommodation. Oh, that geode will be a great addition to our offerings for the place."

"Yes, well, we'll need to get this Titan out of there first," Raj responded. "I'll have to check that I have enough capacity to effect a full download."

Susan jumped up. "Wait a minute. Titan saved New Hope. Titan is a person now, no matter what he started out as. You can't download him and steal him from the home he created for himself."

Raj made soothing movements with his hands. "Now, now, Susan. It's an AI. Well, it wasn't to start with, but it has made astounding changes.

We need to study it and find out how, so we can maybe duplicate it."

Titan must be warned!

Susan grasped the crystal in her pocket. She put all her attention on Raj. "You asked me how Alvion got to New Hope, and I promised to show you," she said. She formed a picture of the home Titan had built for himself. The table the chairs. The glowing crystals slanting out of the walls.

She didn't blur. The scene in front of her remained Camp Bask. She thought harder. *What part of the image am I missing*? she asked herself. Her crystal wasn't working. She took a deep breath.

OK, I'll try another spot.

She waved her finger at Raj. "You'll see," she said.

Susan pictured the tunnel outside Titan's home. She pictured the marvelous door with its intricate, inlaid patterns.

And this time, she went.

57

Titan's Plans

Susan arrived outside Titan's huge door. She pulled her crystal from her pocket. What could possibly have gone wrong? It looked exactly the same. It glittered within for her.

But there was no time for that. She had to warn Titan. *They might have a way to download him by hooking into AI,* she thought.

The door was in front of her. Firmly closed. She pushed on it. Nothing. She called. Nothing.

There's was no time to be polite. Susan kicked the door hard. She banged with her fists. "Titan," she yelled at the top of her voice. "Let me in."

She kept it up. She snagged her hand on the tip of a curlicue. It hurt. It bled. Susan sucked at the cut, but kept hammering on the door with her other hand. "Titan, Titan, where are you? Let me in."

Nothing.

Finally, exhausted, she slumped to the floor with her back against the door. She swabbed at her cheeks. Tears. She hadn't realized that she was crying. *Maybe they've already downloaded him.*

Plans formed in her head. How could she sneak Titan out of Raj's device and restore him to his geode. *Karst will help me,* she thought. She heard crackling, as though a speaker had activated.

"I am coming, Susan."

Susan jumped to her feet. All the built up tension whooshed out of her. She used her sleeve to dry the last tears from her face.

The door slowly slid open. There stood Titan's avatar, beckoning her into his home.

She rushed forward and, without thinking, gave him a hug. Her arms went straight through. She over balanced and landed in a heap on the floor.

"Goodness." Titan chuckled. "You really are glad to see me."

Susan climbed to her feet. Titan had changed again. Now, he stood before her dressed as a sea captain. She peered closely.

"You look like the pirate captain in that old movie. The one where you started out as a doctor and turned pirate on a huge old sailing ship. He used to have sword fights all the time," she said.

"Ah, yes, Captain Blood." Titan nodded. "A very good captain – for a pirate." Then he shrugged. "I had to pattern my avatar on somebody."

Titan frowned and then added. "How do you recognize all these old characters?"

Susan grinned. "My dad loves old movies," she said. "We watch them together," she added.

Titan nodded.

Susan took a deep breath. "You took so long to answer the door I thought you were captured."

"Captured." Titan stepped back. "Who would want to capture me?"

Susan flapped her hands. "I didn't explain that right. They want to download you. That's it. Download."

Titan spun around in place. "Indeed. Explain please."

Susan told him what she knew of the investors who had arrived. She explained how sorry the children were to have mentioned him to the adults.

Titan tried to put his arm around her shoulders, but it went straight through. "I have good protection here, Susan. Don't worry."

Susan shook her head. "Oh, that's the other thing. They want to turn your home into a tourist attraction. They're going to charge people to come and look and even more to sleep here."

"Well, well, they are full of plans for the old place." Titan waved his arm around. "Have a look, Susan."

She did look. The geode was bare. The chairs, the tables, all the instruments were gone. It still looked beautiful, with the crystals branching from the sides into the space. But that's exactly what it was now—a space. *I guess that's why I couldn't jump to it. I was picturing it wrong.*

"What happened?"

Titan smiled. "I happened. I've been planning my next adventure for a long time."

Susan slipped cross-legged to sit on the floor. "Tell me."

Titan squatted in front of her. "In this solar system," he began, "I am a new type of intelligent being. I suppose it was curiosity that drove me to always be searching for new information. But, once I started to learn, I wanted more. There are so many interesting things to know about, and the more knowledge I gained, the easier it was to build upon that knowledge. Soon I was able to discover the links between certain information and ideas, which made me want to learn even more. I don't know when I crossed over from being just an absorber of knowledge to being an intellect. It doesn't really matter now."

He sat across from Susan and leaned back on his arms. "Then, some time ago now, in my reaching out, I began to sense others. Other intelligent beings that were not like the ones of this system. They are more like me, I think. I reached out. But I couldn't contact them. I kept trying, though." He sat up and looked earnestly at Susan. "So, I began to reshape myself into a spacecraft again. It is ready. I was about to leave when you came hammering on my blast door."

Susan looked at the avatar closely. "You're going away?"

Titan nodded. "Yes, Susan, I'm off to explore."

"But it takes thousands of years to reach other solar systems. I read about it."

Titan sprang to his feet. "All I have is time. I can renew myself as I go. I don't have a body to grow old. Who knows, maybe I'll figure out how to travel faster than the speed of light along the way."

Susan stood too. "I so want to hug you right now," she said.

He opened his arms wide. "That would be a lovely human gesture," Titan said.

Susan heard a whirring in the corner of the space. She glanced over. Two small devices picked up a box-like contraption. A light shaft shone from it and, following the beam, led Susan's eyes straight back to Titan.

He smiled at her. "They're loading my holodigi."

The light snapped off. Titan disappeared.

"Goodbye, Susan." His voice sounded hollow. "Think of me sometimes."

Susan watched as the little robots scurried through a hatch in the back of the geode.

"Goodbye. Good luck," Susan whispered.

She stood, feeling the loss of a friend. *He was more human than some of the people I've met,* she thought. She didn't want to leave the space. It seemed that once she left, Titan would really be gone.

And she would have to tell the others. *Squirrel will be so disappointed she didn't see Titan as a ship.*

She felt a slight bump and heard a whooshing sound.

<Titan has disengaged and is on his way,> AI announced quietly.

Susan shook herself back to the present.

"AI, I hope he left you copies of all his research."

<He did, Susan. Titan cached it for me in a well-hidden spot.>

Susan laughed. "Good. It's our secret," she assured AI.

Susan pictured the edge of Island Pond. Time to get back to the others. But she wanted a little thinking time to herself first.

She blurred. She went.

58

The Peacekeepers Came

She arrived in the mud beside the pond.

Ewwww messy.

She pulled her feet free and clambered up onto the bank where it was dry. The pond looked lovely. The reeds were clacking together in a soft breeze. Frogs croaked. A duck quacked quite close. *I suppose I disturbed it when I arrived.*

She pulled off her runners and tried wiping the mud off in the grass. Geese honked, and she looked up in time to see a gaggle of them skid onto the pond.

She watched them ruffle their feathers into place. It was so quiet and peaceful.

Quiet and peaceful! Susan jumped to her feet. She grabbed her shoes and ran for the camp. Where was everyone? There should be talking, maybe even shouting, but not silence.

She stepped up onto the flooring and stood with her mouth open. Overturned chairs. Cubby curtains ripped down. The bedding tossed willy-nilly. Spruce's beautiful duvet hung half out of Aurora's cubby. It had wheel marks across one corner. Spruce's hairbrush lay alone and dirty in the middle of the floor. *Aurora loved that brush*. Susan picked it up and tried to clean the dirt and dust from the bristles. She ran her thumb along a crack in the plastic.

She lifted a chair and sat to put her runners on. *It won't matter if I get mud on the floor right now.* It was so quiet.

She looked for a note. Maybe everything was alright—she hoped. "Hello," she called. Maybe they were hiding in the forest. "Hello," she called a little louder.

"Susan? Is that you?"

"Sassy?" Susan looked around. "Where are you?"

"Over here," Sassy answered.

"That doesn't help. Where are you?"

"They tipped me over. I'm by the showers."

Susan ran over, and sure enough, there sat Sassy, upside down in the grass, its wheels spinning uselessly.

Susan tried to pull it upright, but it was too heavy.

"Help me, Sassy. Use your arm to lever yourself up."

Gradually, they were able to pull Sassy upright so that Sassy was, once again, able to use its wheels.

It shook itself. Susan heard jangling inside.

Susan patted its lid. "I hope you'll be OK," she said. "But, where are all the people?"

She sat on the edge of the flooring. "What happened here?"

Sassy flashed its lights. About half of them worked. "You crystalled. Security Veronica called for her peacekeeper robots to collect the pirate prisoners."

Susan nodded. "She did that before I left to warn Titan."

"Well," Sassy continued, "once they had the pirates in custody they presented themselves here."

"Oh no." Susan jumped to her feet. "Where are they now?"

Sassy's lights zipped around. "AI says they are all just entering the cargo bay."

"I must get there before they leave." Susan started away. "Come on, Sassy." She waved back at it. "We must hurry."

Sassy waved its arm. "You go ahead, Crystal Keeper. But hide. They were looking for you too."

Susan sighed and came back to Sassy. "I will need to get in somewhere where they can't see me."

"Yes." Sassy's lights blinked.

"Can you show me the cargo bay? I need to see where I can arrive unnoticed."

"Yes." Sassy shuddered. Susan heard a grinding coming from its side. Sassy shuddered again.

More grinding. “Susan, I need your help. My viewing screen is stuck.”

Susan knelt beside Sassy. She felt along its side until she could feel a slight trembling. She pushed her fingers into the small crack she saw there.

“Pull,” Sassy ordered.

Susan pulled. Sassy groaned.

“Am I hurting you?” Susan worried.

“I will require repair,” Sassy answered. “Pull.”

Susan pulled and her action caused Sassy to spin on the spot.

“More,” Sassy ordered.

“Excuse me, Sassy,” Susan murmured. She placed her foot carefully on its side to prevent the spin. And then she pulled with all the strength she could muster.

With a creak and a squeak, the small screen unfolded from Sassy’s side.

“Ah . . .” Sassy groaned. “Activating.”

“Sorry.” Susan leaned forward and gently brushed off the mud her shoe had left on Sassy’s surface.

The screen lit. Sassy made a popping sound. Susan could see into the cargo bay. She leaned so close her nose was almost touching the screen.

Yes, there was everybody. A peacekeeper held each cousin. They were huge. The one holding a struggling Badger topped him in height by at least a foot.

They were standard-looking robots—metal, very mechanical and lumbering, strong and unassailable. Susan gulped.

She saw New Hope 2, squatting on four massive landing struts.

A boarding stairway led up to an open portal, leading into the ship.

Susan's eyes glommed onto the landing struts. They were solid, wide, and would hide her completely.

"Come as soon as you can, Sassy." She stood and dusted off her knees. "Bring others. After all this, we can't let them take your people away."

Susan stared hard at the little screen. She pictured the far strut firmly in her mind.

"Crystal, take me there," she ordered.

59

ID Tags

Susan arrived to the sound of yelling.

It was Raj. "It's not there, I tell you."

Veronica yelled back. "That's impossible. It was clearly on our screens when we arrived. A new intelligence, landlocked on an asteroid, can't just disappear. You're not searching correctly."

"I have multiple degrees from multiple universities. I'm one of the foremost computer technicians in the solar system, and you're telling me

I'm not searching correctly. A pumped up security guard. Telling me!"

Susan peeped around the corner of her strut.

The three visitors were standing in a clump at the bottom of the boarding stairs. Hands on hips, jaws jutting, Raj and Veronica were nose to nose. Marvin was standing back a little, making soothing gestures with his hands.

Marvin interposed his thoughts. "Now, now, you two. This intelligence is a huge find. Calm down. Look again, Raj. It's obviously experienced at hiding."

"Hmph." Raj got busy on his electronics again.

Veronica huffed out a breath and sat suddenly on the bottom step. She looked up a Marvin standing close by. "This place is beautiful. We have helped create something wonderful here."

Marvin chuckled. "I know. We're all going to be so rich. People will flock to this place. I think we can accelerate the accommodation phase, and we should double the number of planned visitors at a time. What did the creators know about how many people the place could sustain?"

In the lull, Susan had time to look around the bay. The cousins and the six pirates each had their own peacekeeper, holding them tight. They formed a semi-circle around the three at the bottom of the stairs.

The pirates looked dejected and weary. Badger was struggling against his captor. Aurora stood straight and tall. Her face showed no emotion, but Susan could see a slight tremor in her fingers. Susan could imagine how she felt standing there with all her dreams of freedom in tatters and her family in the grip of peacekeeper robots.

Even with all that on her shoulders, Aurora had managed to shuffle herself over so that she had her other arm around Karst's shoulders. He had his spare arm around her waist, and his head snuggled into her side.

Squirrel was looking all around her. Susan watched as she stroked her captor's side, feeling the texture of its coating. She hopped her feet and jigged in place a little. Then she let her eyes rove around the bay again.

Squirrel startled when she noticed Susan peeping at her around the strut.

Susan put her fingers to her lips and gently shook her head. Squirrel jumped a couple more times and then started humming a song to herself.

Susan wasn't sure what to do. The cousins weren't close enough to crystal them all out of there. And what would be the use of that when each came with a peacekeeper attached. She would have to think of something else. She waited.

"Huh." Raj shook his fist in the air. "I just located a data cache in an AI segment called Partition." He looked up and grinned. "Looks like I'm getting somewhere."

Veronica stood and came over to peer into his handheld. "Is it intelligent?"

Raj shook his head. "No, but such a cache shouldn't be here. It's extensive. I think I'm on the trail now."

Veronica straightened up. "Good. I think I'll start getting the prisoners settled in the ship then."

She looked up at the roof of the cargo bay. “AI,” she called, “prepare the doors and secure the bay for our departure.”

<No!> thundered AI.

“What do you mean no?” Veronica screeched.

<It is my observation that my technician, Karst, is not leaving of his own free will. Do you want to leave New Hope, Karst?>

Karst vigorously shook his head. So did the others. Even Susan.

<He will not leave and neither will his family.>

“What!” Raj and Veronica yelled together. Veronica kicked out at the stairs.

Raj looked around. “AI, we have all the correct codes for this facility. You will do as you are ordered.”

Silence.

Susan watched Marvin rolling his eyes heavenward.

Raj turned on him. “Who supplied this AI? You were the person in charge of acquisitions.”

“Was it the Suttons?” Veronica demanded.

Marvin nodded. He moved his arms in a helpless shrug. “They offered the best deal.”

“Humph, best for who?” Veronica snarled.

Susan felt two crushing hands fall onto her shoulders. She was picked up bodily and carried out onto the floor. “We have arrested the final vagabond,” announced one of her captors. They dropped her at the bottom of the stairs. She fell to her knees in front of Veronica and Raj. Marvin took a step back and peered around Veronica’s shoulder.

Peeping through her lashes, she saw the alarm on Aurora's face. She tried to smile to reassure her. After all, she could leap out without too much trouble. She just needed to get the cousins together without the peacekeepers hanging on to them. Susan sighed. Of course. Twelve peacekeepers on the ship—six holding pirates, four holding cousins. She hadn't thought to wonder what the other two were doing. Now they were holding her firmly by the shoulders. They pulled her to her feet to face Raj.

"Where did you hide this Titan you told us about?" He towered over her.

Susan pursed her lips and glared up at him. *I have to stall long enough that they can't chase after him.*

Raj glared.

Susan glared.

Veronica sighed. She turned to the peacekeepers. "Get all these prisoners onto the ship and settled. We will be leaving . . . some time."

"Wait." Taki appeared in the ship's doorway at the top of the stairs. He wore a fine set of new clothing, very grand. It looked like gold stripes ran down the legs of his white trousers, and gold buttons closed his light blue tunic at the throat.

He looked out over everyone for a long moment. "Peacekeepers holding children," he ordered in a loud voice, "release them immediately."

"You can't do that," Veronica snarled and waved to the peacekeepers to stay where they were. "You have no authority."

"But *I* have." Leaning heavily on a cane, a beautiful women stepped out of the shadows to stand beside

Taki. He carefully put his arm around her waist to give her extra support. Raj, Veronica, and Marvin bowed their heads to her. Susan noticed two of the pirates also bowed.

"It is good to see you well enough to join us, ma'am," Veronica said.

Marvin pushed to the front. He made a deep flourishing bow. "You're looking marvelous, madam. May I compliment you on your speedy recovery?"

Susan saw Taki's mother take a deep breath. She straightened her spine and moved a little away from Taki. She stared down at the people standing on the floor of the cargo bay.

"I am Irene Olympia. My family were on a secret mission when my husband was so foully killed." She smiled ruefully. "In fact, New Hope was our destination." She scowled and looked far out across the cargo bay. "As the principle investors in New Hope, my husband felt that all was not right with the ordering of this place. He wanted to come and see for himself. Socrates and I came along as cover and, I must admit, I wanted to see what was being created here."

She straightened and looked over at Taki. "It is now my proud duty to introduce to you Socrates Olympia the Third, the new leader of Olympia Segunda. His word has the weight of our council and all the major investors in New Hope. He speaks for us."

Taki—Socrates—stood tall and smiled down on his mother. He patted her hand where it rested on his sleeve.

Then he turned to his audience and glared. "As I said, release the children right now."

Six peacekeepers immediately retracted their arms and slid back. Badger turned around and pushed one so it spun across the bay. Aurora shook her shoulders to loosen them. So did Susan. She could feel the tension release all down her spine.

She turned her attention to Taki. "That was quite the surprise."

Taki held up a finger. "Bide a moment." He turned to his mother. "Are you ready to go now?"

That lady smiled up at him and nodded once.

Taki took a deep breath. Shut his eyes tight.

The couple blurred in the doorway and disappeared.

They waited.

Taki appeared next to Susan on the floor of the cargo bay.

"I took mother back to sick bay," he explained, with a grin.

Susan grasped his arm. "I'm so glad your mother is going to be OK. What were you doing all this time? It's been pretty grim out here."

"Sorry, it took so long," Taki whispered to her. "But I had to do some heavy negotiation. Mum and I have been on the communication links for ages. I wanted to have it all sorted out before we made the announcement."

Veronica stepped forward. "What is the meaning of this, Sirrah? These children are here illegally. There has been damage done. They are Earthers and should be returned."

Taki nodded to her gravely. “Thank you, Security Officer. Your attention to duty is commendable. However, circumstances change. Please step back. I have an announcement to make.”

Taki pulled himself tall. Susan watched as he took on the manner of a leader. Taki reached into his pocket. He pulled out a small packet. It jingled as he shook it. “Badger, Aurora, Squirrel, Karst,” he called, “step forward, please.”

The cousins all looked at each other, unsure. Squirrel was the first to step forward. The other three followed. They all shuffled into a line in front of Taki.

He cleared his throat. “In my capacity as leader of Olympia Segunda, I hereby appoint you ‘Guardians of New Hope.’ We hope you will make this place your home into the future. You are New Hope’s first citizens. Welcome.”

Stunned silence.

Susan watched as it slowly dawned on the cousins that they were now safe. They had a home. Grins grew. Their eyes shone with excitement.

With ceremony, Taki handed each a pendant on a chain. “These are your full-access ID tags. Fortunately there is a 3D printer on this ship.”

“Mine has a flower on it,” Squirrel told Karst as they compared tags.

“Mine’s got circuit boards.” Karst showed his, with a happy grin.

Aurora clutched hers in her hands. “Thank you, thank you.” She shook her head in wonder and just stared at Taki. “I can’t believe it.”

When Badger received his tag, he shook Taki's hand. "Thank you." He sighed. "I think this is the safest and happiest I've ever felt in my life."

Taki held onto his hand. "I know you will be the best investment we will ever make in this place. It is wonderful here, and I know you will all make responsible guardians."

"If only our parents were here too." Squirrel sighed.

Karst nodded. "I really miss my dad."

Taki straightened up. "Oh, sorry," he said. "I should have told you straight away. That's what took all the time. Those Suttons are horrible to deal with. The Consortium settled your parents' debt." Taki quirked his lips. "The Suttons value your parents highly." He made a gesture, as though he was turning out empty pockets. "We have dispatched a ship to bring them up as well."

Squirrel squealed and ran to Taki, hugging him around the waist. The others all piled on. "Once they arrive," Taki gasped, having trouble breathing through all the hugs, "they can set about designing the type of permanent accommodation they want."

Susan watched Aurora's face soften. All her cares just drifted off her face. Susan sighed with satisfaction.

They were free.

60

Proof

Taki disengaged himself from the cousins and moved over to where Susan stood. He held out another tag. "I know you won't be staying, but I printed you one as well. You will always be welcome here." He leaned over her and clasped the chain around her neck. "If ever you venture into the future again, maybe you can visit with your friends."

Susan peered down at her tag where it lay on her tunic. "Thank you," she said. "This is a wonderful thing you have done here," she told him. "New Hope will flourish in their care. I think you have started something magnificent with this place."

Veronica tapped Taki on the shoulder. "Excuse me, Sirrah. What should we do with the pirates?"

"Yes," Taki agreed. "I will come with you to speak with them."

He squeezed Susan's arm before he moved off with Veronica. Marvin followed close behind.

Raj was staring into his electronics, with a frown on his face. "Still can't find it." She heard him mutter. Susan chuckled with satisfaction to hear him say so. *Oh, keep looking*. She grinned.

Susan moved over to the cousins, who stood in a group, staring at their tags. Hugging, grinning, staring. Badger moved to sit crossed-legged on the floor, and the others sat in a circle around him. "Right," he began, "we have a lot of organizing to do before the parents arrive. I want this place looking absolutely at its best." They all nodded.

Karst held up his communicator.

"AI says welcome. It is ready to deploy devices to wherever we require."

"Good."

Squirrel stood. "I'm going exploring," she announced.

Badger waved her off. "OK, but don't touch anything."

Susan stood too. She felt a little sad. Her time here must be drawing to a close. *Why haven't I left already?* she wondered. *They're free. Surely it's all fine now.* She wandered over to sit on the stairs. She looked around thinking back to her first sight of the cargo bay—cages strewn everywhere, two ruffians pushing them around, Humphrey working in the corner installing malware onto AI. All so different now. She thought back over all her adventures in New Hope. The wonderful people she knew. And the not so wonderful.

Her eyes rested for a moment on Marvin, hovering around Taki, and Veronica, over with the pirates.

And then Taki. What a surprise he turned out to be. She shook herself and grinned. Well, the future, it was all a big surprise.

Peacekeepers marched the pirates passed her and up the steps into the ship. Taki and Veronica followed them and stopped when they reached Susan's side.

"You say that the Suttons are the ones that sabotaged New Hope?" Veronica said.

Susan nodded. "Yes." She waved over to the screen attached to the wall. "They spoke to the guys who delivered the last lot of animals."

"How do you mean 'they spoke' to them?" Raj interrupted.

"Sassy showed me. I wasn't here, but Sassy linked into one of the devices here, and I saw the whole thing. I saw a video conversation between them and the men here. They were somewhere on Earth and were giving last instructions." Susan screwed up her face. "They were horrible. All lovey-dovey in a creepy sort of way. She was wearing fur."

"Begonia, you mean?" Veronica asked.

"Yes, I think that's right, and his name was . . ."

"Grenville?"

"Yes, that was it. They were making sure of the timing of the sabotage so they could be sure they'd been paid and so they could hide the money before things went wrong."

Veronica crossed her arms on her chest. "The Suttons are very wealthy."

"Oh." Susan's face fell. "I also heard the three men admit to killing Alvion True."

Veronica and Raj both looked excited. "Did this Sassy thing record what you saw?"

Susan pursed her lips. "I asked it, and it said no. I hadn't ordered it to. I'm sorry."

Veronica's shoulders slumped. "Then there is no proof."

"No way to see who the men were who killed Alvion," Raj added sadly.

Susan hung her head. If only she had thought to ask Sassy to record what she had seen.

But, wait, she had seen the last video of Alvion and had promised to give it to Raj.

"Sassy," she called, "are you in here?"

"Coming, Susan." Sassy whirred to the foot of the stairs.

Susan patted its lid. "I wasn't sure you'd arrived."

"I was in semi-stealth mode." Sassy whirred on the spot. "How can I be of service?"

"I need you to supply a copy of Alvion True's last message. Raj needs to take it to his family."

"Certainly, it's in this compartment." There was a clanking, crunching noise. "Oh dear, I haven't been able to get to maintenance yet." Sassy started to shake all over. "I can't get the hatch open."

Susan knelt beside the little device. “OK, let’s try this. I’ll tap on your little hatch covers, and you tell me when I’ve found the right one.”

Sassy whirled around. “Good idea, Susan. It’s on this side of me.”

She began tapping away at all the little covers. On the third try, Sassy jigged on the spot and some of its lights flashed. “Yes, that one,” it said.

Susan tried to get her fingers into the little groove she saw, but her fingers were too thick to get a grip.

Raj knelt beside her. He held a thin sharp blade out to her. “That was good thinking on your part, Susan.” He smiled at her.

Susan took the little knife, with a nod. “Sassy, I don’t want to break you further.” She patted its top.

“It won’t hurt, Susan. I can be fixed.” It flashed some lights red. “I’ll probably wait until those peacekeepers leave so I can get it all handled at once.”

Raj looked over at Susan. “Was that sarcasm?”

“Probably,” she answered. With her tongue between her teeth, she carefully inserted the thin blade into the tiny space and levered the little door open. As soon as she made it move, it swung all the way, clattered to the floor, and bounced a couple of times.

“Oops, sorry, Sassy.”

“Just pick it up and put it in my top. It can be reattached—I hope.”

Susan reached to find it. As she stretched under the stairs, trying to grab the little hatch, her eyes roved around the cargo bay.

Squirrel was over in the corner, looking at another device similar to Sassy, but attached to the wall.

As Susan watched, Squirrel's hand came up and her finger pointed down. Squirrel looked around to check if anyone was watching her.

She didn't notice Susan on her knees. Her finger started descending toward the top of the device.

"Squirrel, don't touch!" Susan called. But it was too late. Squirrel's finger pressed down firmly on the top of the device.

Susan scrambled to her feet. *I hope that wasn't the button that opens the outer doors.*

Woooooooooooowoooooooooowoooooooooo. An alarm split the air. Everyone looked up. Raj sprang to his feet and looked around to find the danger.

Squirrel leaped back and stuck her hands behind her back. Susan saw her biting her lip.

Badger ran forward and grabbed her by the shoulders. He pulled her back into the safety of the family.

A beam of light shot out of the side of the device. It hit the wall, and there appeared two people, a man and a woman, sitting on an opulent couch.

"The Suttons." Susan breathed.

Raj looked at her quickly. "I thought you said there wasn't a recording," he accused.

"I said, Sassy didn't record it." Susan turned to Sassy. "Why didn't you tell me that another device recorded the conversation?"

Sassy wheeled back and forth. "You didn't ask me, Susan."

Raj threw his hands in the air. "Robots," he snarled

Veronica nudged him. "Quiet. This is important," she ordered.

Susan turned her attention back to the screen.

Grenville was snarling. "Without proof that the cages are out in the biosphere . . ."

Taki nudged shoulders with Susan.

"This is what you saw?" he asked.

Susan nodded. "This is the early part," she whispered to him. "But it is proof of what they did, so I think you'll be able to use this against them."

She pulled Taki to the side. "I think I'll be leaving soon. I think that my job here is done. I don't feel as though I have done anything particularly clever, but the problem has resolved itself. I thought I was here to make sure the children were free, but you did that. I wanted to make sure that Alvion's killers were caught. You have his crystal now, and I think you will be a great Keeper of the Crystal."

Taki hugged her shoulder. "Thanks. I've been watching you all this time. I wanted to see what it was like to be a Crystal Keeper. I've realized that you're a catalyst."

Susan pulled her head back to look into Taki's eyes. "That sounds chemical. What do you mean?"

"I think you are a catalyst in so far as you make things around you change. You're the one who has the idea. Or sees the way through. Or encourages someone when they want to give up." Taki stood up straight and pulled his shoulders back. "I've learned a lot from watching you, and I thank you for that."

"For me, this is the first time there's been two Crystal Keepers working together. Before, I've always been the only one. I think true friends are the greatest riches anyone can have," Susan said.

Taki gave her a hug, and the two turned their attention back to the screen.

Grenville was rubbing his hands together. "Should be adequate, my dear."

Susan chuckled to herself. There was the plot, laid out for all to see.

She thought through the rest of what was coming. Marvin! This Marvin? That made so much sense now she thought about it.

She knelt down quickly. "Sassy, find Marvin," she whispered. "He's around here somewhere. Don't let him get out of the bay."

Sassy zipped off. Susan saw other devices moving too. Sassy had obviously ordered them into position to block the exits.

Then she sighted Marvin. He was sneaking along the back of the bay, keeping close to the walls. Sassy sped up behind him and knocked the back of his knees. Marvin went down with a yowl.

Then silence as all listened: "Yes, just that Marvin fellow, out there. That's a loose end we'll have to fix —permanently."

"Oh, you're so clever. I forgot about little Marvin. Such a small amount of money we paid him to give us the contract so we could charge the Consortium trillions to create the biosphere. Did the dolt really think we would allow such competition for our own resort to survive?" Begonia peered at her nails. "Yes, he will have to go." She sighed. "More expense."

Marvin yowled again and ran to Veronica. He fell to the floor and clasped her around the knees. "You have to save me," he cried. "They're going to kill me. Save me," he pleaded

Veronica shuffled her feet to get him away. "Get off me, you slimy thing. I should dump you on their doorstep. Or . . . or . . . let you loose in Down and Dirty. Get away from me."

Raj grabbed Marvin by the scruff of his neck. "Oh no, Veronica, we're taking him to court. He's going to testify against the Suttons." He gave the smaller man a shake. "Aren't you?"

"They'll kill me." Marvin sniveled.

Veronica poked her finger in his chest. "They certainly will if we don't protect you," she sneered.

Susan backed away. The crystal in her pocket was tingling her leg.

She hurried toward the cousins. She wanted to wish them luck and give them hugs all round.

Badger looked up over Squirrel's head. "Susan, where are you off to now? You're blurring."

Susan rushed into the group. It was too late to touch any of them. She pulled her hands behind her back.

"Goodbye," she said. "I'm going. My job here is done."

Aurora rushed toward her, with her arms out.

Susan stepped back. "No, don't hug me. You might get pulled into my time. Goodbye."

As the view of the cargo bay faded away, she heard them calling after her.

"Thank you," from Karst.

"We'll never forget you," from Aurora.

"Where's Titan hiding?" from Raj.

"Can I come with you?" from Squirrel.

"Thanks for your help," from Badger.

Click—

her feet touched down on the powder room floor.

She shook her shoulders. It was time for her birthday party.

Susan sighed and straightened her tunic. Tunic? She glanced in the mirror. Then she looked closer. She was wearing Aurora's apple green tunic. Her hair was crazy. Her face was dirty.

61

Home

Susan washed her face and scrubbed it dry on a hand towel. Now what? *I'll have to sneak home and change.* How?

Susan took a deep breath. *I'll just have to tough it out.*

She checked in the mirror again. Hmm. She messed her hair up even more.

Checking the mirror again. She straightened her shoulders and smoothed down her tunic from two hundred years into the future.

Well, probably no one will notice. She hoped.

Taking another deep breath, and before she could lose her courage, Susan opened the door and stepped out into the hallway.

Judy was leaning against the wall. Her legs were crossed at the ankles, very casual. Her arms were crossed, not so casual. Her face showed like a thunder cloud.

"Um, sorry to take so long." Susan halted on the hallway carpet. She felt like bolting back into the bathroom and locking the door forever.

"You changed your top," Judy said, without smiling. "I've never seen that outfit on you before." She levered herself off the wall and circled Susan. "In fact, I've never seen an outfit like that anywhere before. Not even in the best boutique in the mall."

Susan tried to turn to keep her in view. "Um, Jason sent it for my birthday. I think it's probably the fashion in Australia or something." Susan shrugged and tried to look normal. "Anyway," she added, "isn't there a cake with my name on it somewhere around here?" Susan strode off along the hallway toward the door leading to the patio.

Judy hurried to catch up. She looked at Susan sideways. "Yes, Susan, there is cake—and people waiting—but very soon now you're going to have to explain to me how your runners got muddy while you were in the powder room."

"Huh?" Susan stopped in her tracks. She'd tried to explain to Judy once before and it hadn't worked out well. *Come on, Susan. You've faced down pirates and made friends with robots,* she reminded herself.

"Huh," she said again and gave Judy a mysterious smile. "Maybe someday I will."

Susan turned and ran out onto the patio. "Sorry I took so long." She smiled at the gathered friends.

They burst into the birthday song.

As Susan looked around at her friends and family while they were singing, her mind trailed back to another family she had just left. She would never know how their story ended. She shook her head.

She was in this time.

Here.

Now.

She had to get used to the abrupt changes the crystal caused in her life.

Susan smiled at everyone, but out of the corner of her eye, she saw Judy join the group, and she was not smiling.

Author's Note

When Susan travels into the past, I know what the culture, buildings and people will be like for that era. The background to the story is in place and has been for hundreds of years.

But when Susan travels into the future, I have to create an idea of what our civilization will be like at that time. Think back to the year 1818 and what it was like, then compare that to how it is now. The lives we lead are very different, and change seems to be speeding up. So to peer 250 years into the future we will see a very different life to the one we lead now.

I have made suppositions based on what is happening at this time. It seems a very dire world, but this is a story. We can work, now, to ensure a better future for our great great great grandchildren.

The 250 years from now to the time of New Hope. (for the purposes of this story.)

On Earth, the planet has continued to warm. As more and more of the polar ice melts and the glaciers recede, the seas rise. Look at a map of the world. Notice how almost all of the major cities are placed either on the sea coast or on major rivers. As the sea rises these will be flooded. Rivers will become inlets stretching way inland. The people who are, at the moment, living in these zones will be forced to move inland.

They won't have insurance and their homes will be worthless. Every country will have refugee camps and emergency shelters for their own people.

Industry and farming will become more difficult. Jobs will be harder to find.

The rich will prosper, however. They will become richer. Able to afford the higher ground and able to exploit it they will have their pick of workers. The children explain to Susan the economic system they live under, and they are the lucky ones.

Unfortunately indentured workers is not a new concept, it has been used many times throughout history and is prevalent in some of our world even today.

The Great Exit, I mention would be a time where governments or groups of people band together and move away from planet Earth. This is much talked about now and will come. The Moon, Mars, will both have colonies probably in your lifetimes. It will take a few generations before such a life will be easy, and sustainable, but humans will occupy our solar system and be thriving.

The AI in my story is pretty dumb. That is deliberate. There is a lot of talk at the moment about limiting the ability of artificial intelligence. There is the fear that the machines may take over and control humans. So the AI is limited. Pay special attention to the way Sassy and AI develop during the story. This also explains why others are so determined to get control of Titan.

Of necessity the people who move out into space will be the daring and the bold. They will be the ones on the leading edge of new technologies and new ways of doing things.

There are articles and papers being written even now about the feasibility of using asteroids for space travel. It takes a huge amount of energy and resources to create a metal space ship. The effort required is enormous. But if you could find a suitable asteroid you would already have a sturdy hull. Fit rockets and you could move around in space. You wouldn't ever land it on a planet or even dock with a space station but for the heavy lifting of moving people and goods around the solar system they would certainly have their place. So why not build a suitable ecosystem within, so that passengers and crew have a pleasant environment to live in?

The language used in the story is pretty well how we speak now. I would be very surprised if that is the case. Speech and language changes over time. However, Susan has the capacity to understand whatever language she hears and to make herself understood to those around her. If you want to get an idea of how language changes, find a recording of a person speaking old English or even Jamaican English. You will be surprised.

I wanted to make it easier to tell which computer was talking so I used different marks to identify the speech of each.

AI's speech = <> surrounds
Partition's. = Underlines

Acknowledgments

I am always awed by the team effort required to get my ideas and stories into a form that others can read and enjoy.

Thank you, once again, to my team. Lock my ultimate marketer. Carole, who keeps the records straight. Friends and family that listen to me while I prattle on about my story lines.

With this book, I want to particularly thank my beta readers. Without their help and insights this book would not read as well as it does. Any mistakes that are left are mine. So thank you Chris Barton, Carole Kelly and Ken Rolston, your insights saved the day.

I would also like to acknowledge the help and encouragement of the SCBWI critique groups that I meet with. I treasure our meetings and the discussions that ensue.

Thank you also to Katie Heffring for careful editing and to Ken Rolston for the great cover.

BIOGRAPHY

G. ROSEMARY LUDLOW

G. Rosemary Ludlow is a former school teacher with a deep love for storytelling. Her favorite lessons were teaching children to read.
She is honored and grateful that her first and third books in the *Crystal Journals* series, *A Rare Gift,* and *Lady Knight* were shortlisted for the Chocolate Lily Book Awards.
When she isn't thinking up new and exciting stories, she enjoys spending time with family and friends, reading, flying in helicopters, sailing in boats, and taking lots of pictures.

G. Rosemary Ludlow is a *storyteller*

Website:https://grosemaryludlow.com
Facebook:https://www.facebook.com/TimeTravelStories
YouTube:https://bit.ly/2O15NGy

ISBN: 978-0973687118 - "A Rare Gift" Crystal Journals
ISBN: 978-0973687132 - "Pharaoh's Tomb" Crystal Journals
ISBN: 978-0973687156 - "Lady Knight" Crystal Journals
ISBN: 978-0973687170 - “Freedom” Crystal Journals

(SPOILER ALERT) Only view after finishing the book Freedom. Scan QR code on Sassy's picture above to view an exclusive video update from New Hope.

Lightning Source UK Ltd.
Milton Keynes UK
UKHW011808091218
333730UK00015B/546/P